WORKI

ALSO BY PAUL N. LAZARUS III

THE FILM PRODUCER

WORKING IN FILM

THE MARKETPLACE IN THE '90s

PAUL N. LAZARUS III

ST. MARTIN'S PRESS
NEW YORK

FOR JUDY

A Note on Gender: All references to the male gender in this text are meant to encompass the female gender as well. The motion picture industry has a well-deserved reputation for its less than exemplary treatment of women in most areas of employment. Special mention is made throughout this text of those areas offering particularly good or particularly dismal opportunities for women. While circumstances are unquestionably improving, there is clearly a long way to go.

Design by Diane Stevenson / SNAP•HAUS GRAPHICS

ISBN 0-312-09418-3

First Edition: June 1993

10 9 8 7 6 5 4 3 2

CONTENTS

INTRODUCTION

After years of running a major undergraduate and graduate film program at the University of Miami in Florida, I have become accustomed to the year-end parade of students who make appointments with me and ask the same question: "Now what?" Most are good students whose studies have given them a comprehensive background in motion pictures. Even though they have had a smattering of course work in such practical subjects as producing, screenwriting, editing, and production management, they are curiously unprepared to venture forth into the world and actually get a job.

The motion picture industry is not like many in which representatives of prominent companies visit campuses and recruit the best and the brightest. Indeed, since the very beginnings of the picture business nearly 100 years ago, there have always been more people who wanted positions, at every level, than there have been positions available. This fact alone has created something of a buyer's market, which is at once intimidating and desirable for those on the outside looking in.

Then, too, a training in motion pictures can be put to many good and profitable uses other than the making of feature films in Hollywood. The vast majority of film graduates go on to work in a variety of other related businesses, from commercials to corporate films, from music videos to training films. Very little in the way of information about such activities works its way into a typical film school curriculum.

Those who bring questions to me don't stop with students, present and past. As Florida has in recent years become the third most active production center in America, many people from the community and the state have called for information in the hope of finding a "suitable" position (or simply finding work), acquiring an agent, making a career change, and a host of other related concerns.

Over the years, I have also been impressed by the number of people who simply want to know more about different facets of the motion picture business. Their questions range far afield and are always accompanied by their profuse apologies for taking up time on the telephone when what they really want is a referral to a book that will answer their questions.

Working in Film is an effort to provide just that book. It is meant as a practical resource text for those looking to break into the film industry, in its largest sense, and those seeking to learn a little more about what goes on within it. Inevitably, it is more than addresses and telephone numbers. It reflects many of the conclusions I have drawn from being actively involved in the business for twenty years. During that time, I have functioned as an attorney specializing in copyright and defamation; a business affairs executive for a talent agency; a motion picture talent agent; the head of production for four motion picture studios; the producer of six Hollywood feature films (including *Westworld*, *Capricorn One*, *Hanover Street*, and *Barbarosa*); the founder and CEO of an educational film company; the film commissioner for the state of New Mexico; and now the director of the film program for the University of Miami's School of Communication.

In these various capacities, I have formed opinions or biases which I have endeavored to label as such in my text. (If there were easy answers to such questions as "How do I get an agent?" this book would probably not be necessary in the first place.) While my experience has ranged broadly in the picture business, it certainly has not touched all the bases that this book discusses. I am very grateful to the many persons who have provided insights and advice to me on subjects about which they are expert and I have but a glimmer of understanding. For their time and patience, I am very thankful.

INTRODUCTION

And for those who are contemplating doing something related to motion pictures, it is my sincere hope that this book will prove a useful tool. Some veterans of the movie wars have said to me that the last thing the business needs is a fresh crop of eager job seekers. I strongly disagree. The survival of the picture business as a vibrant and vital medium of communication reaching millions of people all over the globe is directly related to the constant infusion of new talent into the system. This text is an effort to assist that new talent in securing a foothold in the great industry of motion pictures, the industry of making dreams real.

Paul N. Lazarus III
Miami, Florida

PRODUCING

Of all the positions in the motion picture industry, the one least clearly understood is that of producer. Even within the picture industry many people have only a dim understanding of what a producer does. For the outsider, the producer's role is doubly mysterious. In fact, there are many different roles that a producer may perform at all stages of a picture's evolution. Some producers, by background and training or by preference, gravitate to certain functions more than others. Some simply have better skills in some areas rather than in other ones. While these distinctions do exist, the fundamental task confronting any producer is to get a picture made. This may mean securing motion picture rights to a book, developing a script, putting original material together with creative talent such as directors and actors, and most importantly, finding the money to finance the film. Except in those rarest of instances where the producer puts up his own money, when reduced to its essence producing is about *getting movies made*.

Of course, there is much more to the producing game than simply finding the money. But without that, there is nothing further to discuss.

The newcomer looks in vain at the credits of a motion picture to discover answers about producing. On the film itself, or in paid advertising, there will often appear a bewildering array of different producer credits, such as executive producer, producer, co-producer, associate producer, line producer, supervising producer, and senior producer. Such titles provide no clue to what the specific function of the individual involved might have been. Instead, each is a reflection of the particular deal that was negotiated. Each credit reveals, more than anything else, the leverage or clout of the person involved. Perhaps the only objective standard employed is that established by the Academy of Motion Picture Arts and Sciences. That august group has determined that it will give its annual award for Best Picture to the individual (s) holding the credit of producer. Even this is somewhat clouded by the fact that everyone even tangentially involved in an award-winning film rushes to take credit for it.

Actually, the producer wears so many different hats that his job profile comfortably accommodates many disparate personality types from many diverse backgrounds. Entrepreneurial sorts with backgrounds in finance can always find a niche in the picture business. This is to be expected when studio pictures average $26.5 million in cost and even the "smallest" independent picture will be budgeted in excess of $1 million. Those of a more "creative" bent, with training or talent in improving the artistic quality of a project, also fit in easily with the ranks of working producers. So too are effective "numbers crunchers" who can steer a picture on a course of controlled financial management. Even those whose strengths seem to be less *what* they know and more *who* they know find acceptance in a marketplace that is frequently driven by the deal or the creative package that has been assembled for the consideration of a funding source.

It wasn't always this way. When the picture business was in its infancy, early practitioners of the art of producing, such as Thomas Ince, brought great skill and experience to the task at hand. He was able to impose sound business practices on the often outrageous excesses of film production. He deftly balanced the frequently conflicting goals of creative expression and efficient fiscal control. This not inconsequential feat remains at the heart of producing films to this day.

From the 1930s through the 1950s, the heyday of the Hollywood studio system, such producers as Samuel Goldwyn and David O. Selznick were the kings of the jungle. Acting as virtual studios unto themselves, they skillfully orchestrated the production of some of Hollywood's greatest films. There was little doubt in that era that the producer was the lion. It is Selznick, for example, whose name is inextricably linked to *Gone With the Wind*. The director of that classic has become a virtual trivia question. (And all he did was direct not only *Gone With the Wind*, but also *The Wizard of Oz*.)

What, then, does a producer do? In optimal terms, the producer oversees the evolution of a motion picture throughout the process of development, production, and marketing. Since filmmaking is a process—and a collaborative process at that—it is possible to understand the role of the producer by examining how a film comes into being.

At the outset, the producer spearheads what is necessary to position the film for a financing source. This process is known as development. Depending on what stage a project is in when it is conceived of as a film, the producer will take the necessary steps to get it financed. Often the road is a long and tortuous one. If it begins with an idea, or a book, a play, a song, a person's life, or even a breaking news story, then rights to make a motion picture have to be obtained and a screenplay written. All of this costs money. Sometimes the producer will advance his own money in the development phase of the project. Sometimes he will seek money from other quarters, such as a film studio, and dedicate his time and energy to finding the best available (and affordable) screenwriter and then working with him to adapt the property into a script.

The shape of the movie business today is such that most financiers will need to see not only a solid screenplay but also the commitment of a director and star(s). Again, it is the producer who must play the role of the quarterback in moving the project forward toward a financial greenlight or that magical moment when someone agrees to finance the film.

The effective producer, during the development period, must demonstrate significant interpersonal skills if he is to succeed. He must persuade creative types to join his team, financial types to risk their money on his venture, and business types that the project in question is timely and likely to do well in the present marketplace. There is considerable salesmanship required at every stage along the way. It is important that the producer have mastered the language needed to win over such diverse players as actors and studio executives. The more effective the producer is at meeting these challenges, the more likely it is that his projects will get made.

Another important skill in the producer's repertoire during the development phase of a motion picture is balancing creative and commercial tastes. The script must be shaped into a salable vehicle that does justice to the underlying creative concepts while achieving a successful balance in the commercial and financial arenas. This means the producer must stand with one leg in the creative camp and one leg in the business or financial camp.

Once successfully past the development phase of a picture, the producer moves immediately to the rigors of production. Here, he must lead the project through successive stages of preproduction, production, and postproduction. Loosely lumped under the heading of production, these stages of a picture's life are all subject to the producer's leadership and direction. To a greater or lesser extent, his hands are or should be found on the oars that keep the film moving forward both creatively and financially.

When a picture reaches the production stage, many producers find themselves to be fifth wheels. On a movie set, every person, from the director to the craft service person (who makes certain coffee is available and the table is neat), has a specific function to perform. Curiously, this is not the case with the producer. The movie will get made whether he is in attendance or not. This breeds an anxiety level in some producers that leads them to absent themselves from the locations where the pictures are shot. Other producers view production very differently.

In actuality, there is really much that a producer can and should do during production. Most importantly, he should provide the director with a broad perspective, a sense of the larger picture. There is no one else to give such an opinion to the director during production. Every one else connected with the film tends to view the picture from the narrow perspective of his own job. Ask a cameraman how the movie's going and he'll respond in terms of lighting and filters. Ask an actor and he'll give you an extended discourse on his particular role. Only the producer can help the director by providing an overall impression.

There is certainly much more that the producer can do during production. Working with the production manager, he should ride herd on the budget of the film and keep it within the approved financial parameters. He should also assist the director wherever possible in keeping the actors happy and the crew morale at a high level. If it is a studio film, the producer can save the director from having to respond to endless studio questions, thus freeing the director to shoot the picture. These, and many other tasks, are routinely performed by working producers.

Once a film is in production, the producer is in one sense not unlike the manager of a business. He must orchestrate the diverse talents employed in the making of the film and try to reconcile the often competing values of commerce and creativity. Some have described the making of every picture as a war. It certainly does bear similarities to armed conflict. Inevitably there are disagreements, and passions become inflamed. If the producer is able to lead his troops through this campaign, both the artistic integrity of the film and the financial integrity of the budget stand a good chance of being maintained. Skill in crisis management is an important qualification for the adept producer.

The producer who allows his ego or temperament to dictate the outcome of any such dispute makes a serious error in judgment. It is better to avoid conflicts wherever possible, to be sure, but if they prove unavoidable they should be resolved as expeditiously as possible. The easiest and most dependable strategy to follow in resolving such problems in a film is to do what is ultimately best for the picture. This is not as fatuous as it may sound. Rather, it is a principle that rises above jurisdictional arguments or emotional considerations. Thinking in such terms may well provide the producer with a clear indication of the correct course to follow when things get very difficult. As vast sums of money are usually involved in these disputes, the pressures that are brought to bear can be intense. The skilled producer maintains his poise and confidence in such situations and acts in a manner consistent with his assessment of what is in the best interest of the film he is producing.

As the film progresses through postproduction, the editing process solidifies the final shape of the film. Again, the producer is counted on to offer the director and the editor the crucial perspective of objectivity. The producer is mindful of the desired effect that the film is to have on an audience and is aware of the footage that is available to achieve that result. Even after music and sound effects have been added, the producer's voice is sought by the director, who has by now become so close to the film that he has probably lost any real sense of perspective.

Throughout both production and postproduction, the producer remains vitally concerned with the financial status of the film. If the picture is funded independently, outside the studio world, then it is likely that there will be no additional dollars to spend when the budget limit has been reached. It is up to the producer to ensure that the film is completed and ready for distribution with the moneys at hand. If it is a studio picture, there may be more funds available, but only after interminable arguments and perhaps the imposition of financial penalties. As with other aspects of his work, the producer, in his control of the financial side of a film, must balance the seesawing interests of creative efforts and monetary constraints. While this is never easy, it is at the heart of what the producer does.

In time, the film is finished and ready to be turned over to the marketing people in a distribution company. Through their efforts, the film will be "positioned" for release at a certain time of year in a given number of theaters. The producer who walks away from his film at this juncture, believing in the "trust me, kid" assurances of the distributor, does so at great risk to his film. Distribution companies often release more than twenty-five films a year. They are unable to put their full weight and resources behind each of these releases. This imposes on the producer the task of being the chief advocate for his film—at all costs. Untold numbers of films have been sacrificed before the public ever had a chance to render a judgment—simply through inept or inefficient handling by marketers. It is up to the producer to use all diligence to ensure that this doesn't happen to his film.

For his efforts in producing a motion picture, the producer is generally compensated quite handsomely. He does not receive the multimillion-dollar fees that today's actors or directors are receiving, but he is still rewarded very well. He can expect to earn somewhere between $150,000 and $750,000 for producing one film. In addition, he will receive "points" in the film, which are percentages of net profits (one point equaling 1 percent of the net profits). The computation and distribution of a film's net profits are the subject of much controversy in Hollywood, particularly today, with the much publicized suit brought against Paramount Pictures Corporation in connection with the film *Coming to America*. The present brouhaha surrounding the accounting systems employed by the major distribution companies stems from the fact that if the picture is a big enough hit, the points will have a very significant meaning. In this regard, it should be remembered that the profits, if any, from a motion picture are derived not simply from theatrical revenues, but from revenues from all sources—from videocassettes to television, from soundtrack royalties to merchandising royalties.

It is certainly possible to earn a great deal of money as a film producer. However, as one observer of the passing scene noted, while you can make lots of money it is nearly impossible to earn a living. This is a point worth noting. The big money comes when the film is actually produced. In development, the producer receives a comparatively minor sum to supervise the project.

ally his development fees are insufficient to keep his foreign ıed and his restaurant bills current. There is thus consider- ressure on the producer to get his films made. Sometimes oducer is hot and everything falls neatly into place. There ther times when projects, for whatever the reason, don't k out. Those are the tough times for a producer, and almost ery veteran has gone through them. As with most businesses, ıccess seems to be cyclical. It therefore behooves the producer o make allowances for the bad times.

With only a handful of exceptions, the status of the producer today has fallen precipitously from the halcyon days many years ago. Today, it is the commitment of a director or an actor to a project that attracts the funding of a studio—not the commitment of a producer. For the most part, since they are considered interchangeable by the studios, producers will generally lose any disagreement between themselves and a star or a director that is mediated by a studio. The case is significantly different if the producer has put together a picture with independent backing, because in that situation the producer is in the power seat. It can be brutally difficult to raise the funds necessary to make a film. The rewards for the producer are great, however. He will enjoy far more creative control in the making of an independent picture than he would with a studio film, and he is much more likely to be able to structure a better deal for the picture's distribution after the picture is completed. Such an arrangement will probably make the producer's contingent compensation, his percentage of profits, that much more meaningful.

If this is what a producer does, then, how does one get to be a producer? There are no examinations like medical boards or law boards to pass—although perhaps this is not such a bad idea. No license must be obtained to call yourself a producer. On the contrary, it is simplicity itself. One announces he is a producer, and in the eyes of the world, he is a producer. Whether he can then get a movie made, or know what to do if he is fortunate enough to do so, is quite another question. Education is, as with most pursuits in life, a reasonable way to start. Most undergraduate and graduate film programs in this country offer at least one course in producing. Depending on the expertise of the instructor, this can be a fair way to begin. Perhaps the most extensive training, in an educational context, can be gotten from the Peter Stark Motion Picture Producing Program, a part of the School of Cinema–Television at the University of Southern California in Los Angeles.

The Peter Stark Program is a two-year (four semester) graduate program aimed at training students "as creative independent motion picture producers or as operating executives in motion picture and television companies." It admits approximately thirty students each fall and awards a master of fine arts (M.F.A.) degree on successful completion of the program. Named for the son of noted film producer Ray Stark, this program offers a comprehensive examination of the motion picture industry, from exhibition to distribution to the nuts and bolts of producing. In lieu of a thesis, the program requires a fully developed film project and marketing plan.

Inquiries regarding this program should be directed to the Peter Stark Program, USC School of Cinema–Television, University Park, Los Angeles, CA 90089-2211. Telephone: (213) 740-3304.

For the student looking for a self-help approach, this author has published a comprehensive work on the subject. (See, Lazarus III, Paul N. *The Film Producer.* New York: St. Martin's, 1992.)

Of course, a formal education is but one way to achieve the goal of becoming a producer. It should be noted that while education may better prepare the beginning producer for his profession, it does not secure him a position as a producer in the real world. That can come only by dint of his own efforts. Over the years, experience has shown that several occupations provide unique experiences that seem to segue well into producing. Talent agents and personal managers learn, in the course of repre-

creative talent, such basic skills as making deals and g with artists. Both talents are invaluable for a producer ess. Further, they make all-important contacts throughout ertainment industry. It must never be overlooked that the industry is a "people" industry. The more people one s, the easier it is to get things accomplished. To the outsider approaches Southern California for the first time, the walls rounding the picture business can seem virtually impregnable. et they can be breached. They have been many times before.

Another way for the aspiring producer to establish a foothold in the industry is to seek an entry-level job in the creative ranks of a studio. Usually such jobs range from being a reader (the person who first looks at submitted literary material, synopsizes it, and offers his recommendation on it), to being an assistant for a production executive, to working in some aspect of creative affairs where pitches are heard, writers worked with, and projects supervised. These positions are considered very desirable because they pay weekly salaries, with all the usual corporate perquisites and benefits, and are excellent stepping-stones toward the higher echelons of the industry, including producing. While correspondingly difficult to obtain, these positions still have enough turnover to make them reasonable goals for which to shoot.

Then, too, the fledgling producer can always seek employment with a more experienced producer. The most successful producers themselves operate like mini-studios. They have development people working for them who read; work with writers; solicit new material from literary agents; cover new books, plays, and magazine articles; and, in general, perform all the tasks that are done at the big studios. Often the working conditions can be very informal, and although the hours will be long, the work is typically very enjoyable.

Since producing incorporates so many different skills and talents, many other professions can be considered as worthwhile training grounds for producers. The legal profession, public relations, publishing, or for that matter virtually any kind of solid business background, will unquestionably prove helpful to a producer. Obviously, the more closely aligned to producing that another business is, the better it will serve the aspiring producer.

The most obvious approach of all should never be discounted. If the new producer finds a property that he feels is a wonderful movie opportunity, he can always bring it to a more experienced producer and join forces with him. Many a producer got started in the industry by teaming up with someone with much more clout the first time out. This arrangement will prove beneficial to both parties. The beginning producer will be able to ride on the coattails of the experienced producer and learn from him in an on-the-job educational situation. Happily, he will also be paid for this learning experience. For the experienced producer, it may be that rare circumstance where a project that he didn't have to discover and nurture drops into his lap. This is not a time for the new producer to turn greedy. While he may receive less compensation under this arrangement than he would if he were producing alone, it should not be forgotten that some piece of the pie is better than nothing. And it is a beginning, a first step, and most assuredly not a business arrangement that is forever carved in stone.

It has been said that the hallmark of a good producer is someone who puts together a film that breaks new ground and is the first film of its kind, or someone who takes a familiar concept and executes it best. These two criteria, being first and being best, are goals toward which everyone should strive. A moment's reflection, however, will indicate that such accomplishments are more the exception than the rule. While no one sets out to make a bad film, the truth of the matter is that very few films either aspire to or achieve the highest level of art. This is understandable in a system organized around the profit motive. Films like the *Rambo* series certainly wouldn't constitute high art in the opinion of the majority. Yet they made significant contributions to the coffers of all concerned—profits that facilitated the making of nore films—and brought entertainment to millions of peo- over the world.

ıch considerations as these lead to the issue of what consti- ı good producer and what should be his philosophy of king. Beyond the technical skills that a good producer bring to the table is the philosophy he evolves to govern ıy-to-day decision making. In the art of deal making, for ıple, some practitioners prefer to push as hard as the leverage ıe situation permits. They are happiest when they have taken eir advantage as far as possible and soundly defeated the party n the other side of the table. Other deal makers are far more comfortable finding a middle position at which both parties give and take in some measure and come away feeling good about the negotiation. It is difficult to pass judgment on which system or operative philosophy is better. In the final analysis, it depends on the comfort level of the individuals involved.

The same can be said of the working philosophy for producers. Some producers have a multitude of projects in the works at all times. They understand that pictures are often made for the most serendipitous of reasons and that their best strategy should be to juggle as many projects as possible, hoping always that some will get made. Other producers are very uncomfortable with a shotgun-type approach and prefer instead to put all of their energies behind one or two projects to which they are deeply committed. Both systems are operative and both have numerous producers who subscribe to them. It should be added that neither is a sure road to success.

My own philosophy as a producer was to favor those projects that suggested films I myself wanted to see. Since my personal tastes have always run toward quirky, off-center films, I was more disposed to expending my producing energies developing and selling projects of that kind. Admittedly, it would have been simpler to stick closer to the middle of road, but my passions were best directed to those subjects about which I felt most strongly. Is a project a good one because it sells? Or is it good when you feel in your heart of hearts that it reaches a standard of high quality? Again, these are questions that defy facile answers. They are highly relevant for the producer, however, who is charting his career and endeavoring to figure out where best to put his energies.

One inescapable conclusion is that the hard work needed to see a project get made demands real passion from the producer. Whether that passion arises from a profound belief in the project or from a belief in its salability is not a question that need be answered. The individual producer will work that out for himself. The competition to get pictures made is so rigorous that the producer must approach this task with great passion, persistence, and patience. There will be many more setbacks than there will be triumphs. It is always easier to rally from the setbacks if you remain committed.

If the producer is able to pick himself up after repeated rejections and keep on trying, secure in the belief that his judgment will one day be validated, then he can indeed consider himself a working professional. Often his faith and judgment will be rewarded by the events that finally come to pass. *Westworld,* the first studio film that I produced, was turned down by eight studios in succession. The ninth and last studio to see it, MGM, took it on more for its low cost than for any belief in the project. The film itself, executed as its writer-director Michael Crichton had said it would be executed, proved to be the most profitable picture made in that MGM administration's regime. This indicates that the eight studios who passed on *Westworld* had no window into the future, and it demonstrates the need for persistence on the part of the filmmakers. Producers make their movies using other people's money. Rarely will this money be made readily available to them. The producer needs staying power to play the game over the long haul. A sincere belief in the viability of the project he is trying to sell is a source of both comfort and inspiration in this process.

The marketplace for the producer today is considered

than it has been in recent years. In all probability, this duct of the swollen films budgets and the costs of prints ertising, which today aggregate nearly $35 million. While vords are spoken about the wisdom of cutting back on y costs and otherwise affecting economies within the sys- ie fact is that picture budgets continue to spiral upward. than ever, this puts the big companies into a game where have to shoot for the big stakes every time out. Modest its from modest films are of little use. So great are the re- irces committed by these companies that they have to swing r the fences with every picture they make.

The inclination of the big studios today is to avoid development costs wherever possible. Such costs typically involve the expense of readying a film for production. It is very common for hundreds of thousands of dollars to be spent acquiring rights to make a film and paying to have a screenplay written. This, in turn, places great pressure on the producer to find the means somehow to develop his pictures for the marketplace. Well-heeled suppliers such as Interscope, Imagine, and Morgan Creek have sprung up to help fill that void. They will carry the development cost load up to, and often including, a portion of the cost of actually producing the film. Through one arrangement or another, they will then team up with the major studios to have the film distributed. In essence, they are partners with shared risks and shared benefits.

But what of the independent producer? Never truly independent to begin with, he finds himself in a constant struggle to raise development funds in order to have pictures that can be considered for production by the big companies. Often today, an idea with a writer attached is not enough to induce a studio to spring for development money. Where, they ask, is the director or the star who will theoretically hedge a portion of the development risk by assisting in the project's development? What is the track record of the writer? How many successful films has he written? And how recently? This line of questioning will inevitably impinge upon the freewheeling development posture of many film producers. Money is tighter in the marketplace, and the producers must adapt accordingly.

While that speaks to the fashion of the times, it is also true that films continue to be made and projects continue to be developed. The history of the film business reveals that the business follows a cyclical pattern of good times and bad. There are periods of wild inflationary spirals and times of retrenchment. Pictures continue to be made, however, and they continue to have producers, of one stripe or another, at the helm. The qualities of a good producer have not changed markedly over the years. He will still bring persistence and patience to his labors. More than anything else, he will bring a passion to his work. While characteristic of most of the job categories within the picture business, this dedication may be especially necessary for producers because of the entrepreneurial nature of their tasks. If the aspiring producer does not find that passion within himself, he is well advised to seek some other avenue of employment.

Producing is a rigorous but rewarding profession. It frequently demands tremendous inner resources and strengths. If that passion for films and the dedication to keep working for the goals one wants to achieve are not present, the road ahead will prove very long indeed. But with that passion, everything is achievable and within the grasp of anyone willing to work hard for it.

DIRECTING

Mother Teresa stood before the Pope. Before she took her leave, the Pope asked her if the Church could do anything to commemorate her many years of service and good works. She shook her head. "Anything at all," the Pope continued. "Perhaps we could name a hospital or an orphanage after you." Still, Mother Teresa shook her head. "Think it over," the Pope said, "I will do anything in my power to grant you that which you would like." Mother Teresa began to leave the room. Suddenly, she turned back to face the Pope. "There is one thing," she stated. "What is that?" the Pope replied. "I would like to direct."

It will come as no great surprise to learn that the director's chair is the most coveted seat in the motion picture industry. More people aspire to fill that position than any other in front of the camera, behind the camera, or in the executive suite. This may be attributed to a single facet of the director's work—control. With the myriad decisions that he must make, and with the number of times that he has the final say on creative matters, the director has a unique opportunity to shape the final product that will appear on the screen.

The business need not be structured in this way. In earlier times, the producer enjoyed far greater control over the creative process. In television today, it is the producer-writer whose creative mark is indelibly impressed upon the product, far more than that of the director. In the medium of motion pictures, however, it is the director who stands tallest.

This fact often frustrates other creative individuals involved in the production of a movie. It is very difficult for the screenwriter, for example, to turn over his original work to a director who will proceed to "interpret" it as he sees fit. Every aspect of the film, from the motivation of the characters to the camera angles on each take, becomes the province and responsibility of the director. This became abundantly clear in the 1950s and 1960s when French filmmakers and theorists developed the thesis that the director is the *auteur*, or author, of a film. His unique quality was thought to define the shape of the film above the efforts of the screenwriter or anyone else involved in this collaborative medium. Indeed, those directors whose work lacked distinctive attributes were often considered less worthy than their peers who evinced a more individualized technique.

While there has been a modest retreat from the *auteur* theory, it continues to carry considerable weight in the 1990s. Filmmakers like Woody Allen, Robert Altman, and Alan Rudolph typify the kind of director usually thought to be representative of the *auteur* attitude.

More generally today, writers, producers, or actors turn to directing to effect greater control over their work. Examples abound. Actors from Kevin Costner to Jodie Foster, from Sean Penn to Emilio Estevez, from Clint Eastwood to Barbra Steisand, even Warren Beatty, have all taken the directorial reins when their popularity (and thus their business leverage) permitted. It is the same with writers and producers. When questioned as to why they chose to expand their creative horizons into directing, most have said the same thing—to achieve more control.

Control is asserted over the process from the moment the director is hired. It extends throughout the life of the film, from preproduction to production to postproduction. During the preproduction period, the director will oversee the final polish on the script, tilting it or modifying it to suit his sensibilities. Director Paul Verhoeven's recent attempts to modify the screenplay of *Basic Instinct*—which fetched its author, Joe Eszterhas, a record price of $3 million—have been well documented in the movie press. The screenwriter fought for what he felt was the "integrity" of the script, while the director (apparently supported by the star, Michael Douglas) fought to adapt the screenplay to his own vision.

Casting the film, while also subject to the influence of the people putting up the film's finances, is likewise an area where the director's presence will be felt strongly. Crewing the picture, especially with important key positions such as cinematographer, editor, composer, production designer or art director, and first assistant director, is similarly determined in large part by the director. Significantly, those members of the crew who are most concerned with keeping track of the expenditure of funds—the production manager, the auditor, and even the completion guarantor—are rarely selected by the director. His main focus is on matters creative rather than financial.

Inevitably, the creative side of a picture will dovetail into the financial side. The director, of course, will select the film's locations. Should he wish to move a California-based show to New York for two weeks of location work, the cost factor will have to be faced. There may be only enough money to shoot on the "New York street" of a studio backlot, in which case the financial interest will usually hold sway, and it will probably be the director who must give ground. Or, if the director would like three days to shoot the love scene so as to bring his many creative notions into play, but the schedule will permit only a day and a half, again, at least in preproduction, the director will reluctantly accede to the wishes of the money people. He does so knowing that during production he will have several more bites at the apple before finally giving in.

Throughout preproduction, the department heads bring all of their creative questions to the director for a decision. What colors will the living room be done in? What kind of dress will the leading lady wear? What weapon will the bad guy use? Every conceivable item that will show up in a frame of the movie is subject to the director's approval. He will expect his department heads to offer him choices from which he will make final decisions. Down the road, he may have to work out some minor bumps with the star in terms of wardrobe, hairstyles, and the like, but in the end it is the director who makes the final determinations.

It is more of the same during production. On a fundamental level, it is the director who yells "Action!" and "Cut!" It is the director who decides when the coverage of a scene is sufficient, when the performances have attained the desired levels, and when there are enough angles filmed to cut the picture successfully. It is a vast undertaking which must focus at once on the overall thrust of the story and characters and on the minutiae of untold thousands of details affecting all aspects of the production.

As production continues, the director will have the opportunity to view the result of his work at a screening of the previous day's dailies. Other than the producer—if he is present—the director will typically be the only person at the screening with a perspective on the whole forest, and not simply the individual trees. Actors see only themselves; cinematographers see the lighting; art directors, the physical trappings; and so on. This puts continual pressure on the director to maintain his "vision" of the production. If that vision warps or wavers, the results, as seen in the finished film, will likely be calamitous.

When production has concluded, the director turns his attention to postproduction. Technically, getting back processed film each day and syncing up the dailies (putting the picture and sound reels in alignment) is a postproduction procedure. It is generally thought, however, that post begins when principal photography has wrapped. The director begins his cut of the picture after the editor has completed assembling the film. The director then completes the rough cut, working closely with the editor. Although creative disagreements are common in this situation, both sides are aware that the director has the final word.

The composer will do his work under the close supervision of the director, as will the sound effects editors and all of the technicians who make up the postproduction team. There will be many suggestions made, but as before it is the director who quarterbacks this effort. The Academy of Motion Picture Arts and

Sciences makes an effort to recognize the achievements of the highly skilled and marvelously creative men and women who work with the director in postproduction by awarding Oscars each year in all of their fields.

The public and the overwhelming majority of the industry accord credit (and blame) for the finished film to the director. Looked at in this manner, the director who delivers a critically well-received commercial hit will garner wide industry praise. If the picture gets good notices, but does disappointing business, the director can still emerge unscathed. It is only when the film is panned by the critics and also fails at the box office that the director will be held responsible for everything. Technical credits are of no real importance if no one comes to see the picture. If the movie fails, the director must accept the responsibility.

At every stage, whether working with the editor to determine where a certain cut will be made, or determining with the composer when a given music cue will end, or setting the levels of dialogue, music, and effects at the sound mix, it is the director who makes the final decision. If he is open to suggestions and listens to his crew, he may pick and choose from a number of interesting options. If he is closed to this kind of proffered assistance, the picture will end up being whatever he wants it to be. Such is the power of the director today, and such is his control over the process.

Inevitably, certain directors refine their skills so as to demonstrate particular prowess at one or more film genres or types. Some develop a "feel" for action-adventure, others for character stories, and still others for comedy. Only a rare few have the all-encompassing skill to be equally proficient at all kinds of films. At this time, the shortest list of sought-after directors is in the area of comedy. Perhaps, as actors have always maintained, this is because comedy is the most difficult genre of all. Maybe it is because television develops directors who are skilled in the three-camera sitcom format, which bears little resemblance to a one-camera motion picture shoot. In any event, as long as comedy continues to thrive at the box office, the motion picture industry will always be on the lookout for promising directors of comedy.

While not always as hot from the standpoint of studio interest (based presumably on the difficulty of casting), there is also a real need in the marketplace for a skillful director of character-driven stories. This is the main calling card of a director like Barry Levinson (*Rainman, Avalon, Tin Men*, and *The Natural.*)

For the director, as for the actor, there is a real danger in being typecast. It is gratifying and profitable to be a director in demand, but if you are typed in a narrow niche, it can be somewhat stultifying as well. For this reason, "hot" directors, which means those directors who have directed a film that is doing well at the box office, often seek to expand their horizons by moving into another genre entirely. It is certainly no stigma to end up as a master of one kind of film, but many in the creative community work hard to avoid that kind of label.

In addition to the kinds of films that a director has made, knowledgeable insiders will want to know whether he has worked with big stars before. Directing a superstar who is receiving anywhere from $5 million to $15 million can be a truly harrowing experience. Temperament has a way of replacing professionalism on the set. Many a director has fallen victim to the outrageous demands of an actor who has the studio in his corner for fear the actor will otherwise cost the studio huge sums in production overages. Many of the biggest stars routinely get approval of the director in their contracts. The most frequently used yardsticks for granting that approval are the successful films the director has done, and the other big stars he has worked with in the past. This can quickly get into a cart and horse dilemma for the promising director and will remain so until some star is willing to take a chance and work with him.

And now, the $64,000 question: How do you get to be a director? Would that there were an easy answer to this question. There is not. There are many routes that have been successfully (and unsuccessfully) followed in the past. The critical stumbling block is that it is very difficult to showcase your talents because the cost of films is so great. Actors can work in neighborhood playhouses and fight to get agents and casting people to see them do their stuff. With talent, persistence, and passion for their craft, they will probably get at least a chance to prove what they can do. It is not the same with aspiring directors. Most new directors do not break in on a studio film. Since the cost of studio pictures has risen in excess of $28 million, this is hardly a surprise. But even small independent films require hundreds of thousands of dollars to make. Given the problems of finding financing for a film, it is a testament to the resourcefulness of an aspiring director that he ever gets his chance to direct.

One place to begin for those interested in directing is through the Directors Guild of America. This organization is the collective bargaining agent for not only directors, but also unit production managers, assistant directors in film, and technical coordinators, stage managers, associate directors, and production associates in tape. The strength of the guild is derived from the fact that the major motion picture studios and many of the large companies that produce films are signatory to the guild's Basic Agreement and have agreed to be bound by all of its terms and conditions. This agreement speaks to such issues as minimum salaries, residuals, compensation, credits, and working conditions. Among many other items covered is the all-important right of the director to do the first cut of a motion picture—and to be free to do it without interference from any financing party. Those employers who are signatory of the agreement must contribute to pension and welfare plans as well as to health benefits for the guild membership. The guild maintains principal offices in New York and Los Angeles and has representatives in all of the major production centers around the country.

The Directors Guild has an Assistant Directors Training Program that has provided many with their first taste of working in production. The program requires a bachelor's degree or two years of practical experience in film or television production.

There is a wide-ranging testing process that examines verbal and mathematical skills, as well as abilities in problem solving and personal interaction. The applicants are narrowed down by a process of grading and assessment, with the finalists being personally interviewed. The number chosen each year is partially dependent on industry needs. If chosen, the successful candidate will undertake a structured apprentice program that will include actual time working on-site during production. His time will be spent rotating among a number of different shows, not always on consecutive days. Seminars are also held to provide firsthand lessons from active members of the guild.

The training program offers a fine entry-level position for someone starting out in the picture business. The tasks given program participants, or even those who work their way up to being assistant directors, have little to do with actually directing a film, however. They focus upon the paperwork and the practical problem solving that must be done in the operation of a motion picture set. Such tasks are invaluable and can provide very worthwhile experience, but arguably do not move anyone closer to directing a film. Indeed, other than what one gleans informally, there is next to no emphasis placed in the program on the aesthetic or creative problems with which all directors must wrestle.

For the would-be director who does not know many people in the industry, the program can be invaluable in beginning the process of networking among industry professionals. It can also provide valuable exposure to the operation of a set and an inside view of the dynamics of making a film. These are all worthwhile lessons to learn. It should be understood, however, that it is very rare for unit production managers or even first assistant directors to make the transition into directing a picture. There is no pattern of moving up through the ranks to become a director one day, as if you were moving through the ranks of a corporation and hoped one day to sit in the president's chair. For the right person, this program offers a first-rate entry-level position and is well worth the expenditure of effort it takes to go through the selection process.

Further information about both the New York and the Los Angeles programs can be obtained from the following addresses:

Administrator
Assistant Directors Training Program
110 West 57th Street, 2nd Floor
New York, New York 10019

Administrator
Assistant Directors Training Program
14144 Ventura Boulevard, Suite 270
Sherman Oaks, California 91423

For the student seeking more information on the subject of directing, many texts have been written describing how directors work and what makes the great ones great. A good sample of these books includes:

Braudy, Leo and Morris Dickstein, eds. *Great Film Directors: A Critical Anthology*. New York: Oxford University Press, 1988.

Giannetti, Joseph. *The Film Director as Superstar*. Garden City, N.Y.: Anchor Press, 1970.

Katz, Steven D. *Directing: Shot by Shot*. Los Angeles: Lone Eagle Publishing Company, 1991.

There are certainly other paths that have been followed in search of the opportunity to direct feature films. Many have attempted to make this transition after prior success in other motion picture job categories. In today's marketplace, this is most readily accomplished when one is a successful screenwriter. The frustrations that the screenwriter feels have already been cited. To overcome them, all the screenwriter of today need do is be responsible for writing two commercially successful films. The writer will then bask in the sweet glow of being considered hot. If he decides that he will sell his next writing effort only to a studio that will allow him to direct, the chances are excellent that his strategy will prove successful. Little thought will be expended as to whether the writer has the right stuff to be a director. The system will swing in his favor out of the insatiable appetite it has for commercial success.

Other routes to directing are somewhat more problematic. Producers with enough muscle or clout can shoehorn themselves into a directing role simply through their connections and knowledge of how the game of moviemaking is played. There are numerous instances of this today, from Larry Turman to Irwin Winkler, from Stanley Jaffe to Art Linson. On occasion, as with Stanley Kramer and Alan Pakula, the results have been exciting and worthwhile. More often, the resulting films have lacked significant artistic or commercial success. This fact offers the most definitive answer about the compatibility of these two positions. The aesthetics for the successful producer are far from the aesthetics for the director—regardless of the muscle the producer can employ or his intimacy with the deal-making process.

Other technical people have also coveted the director's chair and at a successful stage in their lives endeavored to try it out. More cinematographers and editors—both craftsmen who work in close proximity to the director—have probably attempted directing than any other group. Interestingly, cinematographers have fared considerably less well than have editors. Such distinguished directors as Robert Wise, Hal Ashby, and Karel Reisz all began as editors before becoming important and very successful directors. When the shift was attempted by cinematographers, such as William Fraker, Haskell Wexler, or Bill Butler, the results were less impressive.

Maybe this is an area where common sense provides the

surest answers. Successful movies, at least from the standpoint of an audience, are those that capture the imagination, that involve the audience in the story being told and the characters that are seen and heard. Shooting beautiful pictures is fine, but it is very much the icing on the cake. Without a sure hand in directing the actors in the telling of the story, and without the knowledge of how a screenplay "works" so as to get it on the screen, the director is most unlikely to score many points with today's audiences. The editor seems better equipped to achieve these ends than does the cinematographer.

Still another opportunity for the aspiring director to seize is the "audition" film shot in one of the many film programs in colleges and universities around the country. More will be said about film education in a later chapter, but for this purpose it is certainly worth mentioning that there have been success stories of directors getting their start on the basis of student films. George Lucas, for example, shot what was essentially a "pilot" for his first feature, *THX-1138*, while still an undergraduate at the University of Southern California. Other directors, such as Robert Zemeckis, Spike Lee, and Michael Dinner, have similarly made the immediate transition into feature films on the basis of their student work. The odds against this happening are very long, however. It is more likely that the graduate of a film program will have received a good grounding in the fundamentals of filmmaking and then seek some form of entry-level position. The road to feature film directing can also be pursued by starting out in television. Such directors as Michael Crichton and Peter Hyams began their directorial careers by writing and directing "Movies of the Week" for network television. Thus, early in their careers, they established a track record of being able to deliver films on time and on budget. These considerations were extremely important in the minds of financiers pondering giving these individuals their shot at directing their first feature. Of course, it didn't hurt that both Crichton and Hyams had wedged their feet firmly in the door of both television and motion pictures by being able to write their own material. Likewise, the estimable James L. Brooks cut his teeth in the television medium, where he still maintains an active presence, before adding motion pictures to his résumé.

From a technical standpoint, different directors bring different skills to the table. Some directors are deservedly known as actors' directors. By that, it is meant that they possess a grasp of how to communicate with actors and help the actor shape his performance. This may be done through long discussions with the actor, or, as with the late John Huston, with minimal dialogue between director and actor. It is certainly useful if the director has had formal training as an actor, but experience indicates that it is by no means essential.

Some directors carry their love for the technology involved to the ultimate end of mastering the craft of cinematography. Director Peter Hyams successfully petitioned his way into the cinematographers' branch of I.A.T.S.E. (International Alliance of Theatrical Stage Employees) and doubles as cinematographer on the films he directs. He contends that it is for him the most efficient and effective way to get his particular vision of the film from his head to the screen. Most directors prefer the collaborative aspects of working with a cinematographer, regardless of their personal knowledge.

The more emphasis that is placed on control of the technical aspects of a film, the closer the focus moves to a director's personal style. The restless, busy camera that Martin Scorsese favors, the visual pyrotechnics that characterize many of the films of Brian De Palma, these and like tendencies can be seen as the signature of a certain director. Film theorists have pondered whether these qualities that get close to authorship of films should command more respect than the work of a director like Sydney Pollack, whose films may be described as more "commercial." For the director starting out, a sense of personal "style" may appear absurdly out of reach. Yet the more opportunity the director actually has to direct, the more likely it is that such a personal style will evolve.

A personality trait not often discussed but of critical importance for a director is the ability to make decisions quickly and definitively. Sometimes arriving at decisions is extremely difficult for an individual, and this can have a disastrous impact on the budget of a movie and the morale of a crew. One Academy Award–winning director has a very difficult time reaching decisions on everything from locations to set dressing. This paralyzes the crew, who must await final word from the director before locking things down. The director's inability to render timely decisions forces contingency plans into existence and creates inevitable budget overages.

Looked at from this perspective, directing a film is a vast exercise in the deployment of resources and personnel, not unlike a military campaign. Procrastination can spell utter defeat for both enterprises. The lines of authority are clear. The decisions must be made in a timely fashion, and the overwhelming number of those decisions must of course be correct.

If the production of a movie gets into difficulty, the film media are drawn to it like sharks in a feeding frenzy. The public seems to have an endless fascination with the amount of money that can be spent when a picture spins out of control. Usually this is the fault of the director, although frequently, extenuating circumstances such as weather, death or incapacity of the star, or some similar hardship may materially affect production. Much has been written about such runaway budget films as Michael Cimino's *Heaven's Gate* and Brian De Palma's *The Bonfire of the Vanities*. When a budget is greatly exceeded during production, it is highly unlikely that a director is seeking to punish the financing source for some perceived wrong. Rather, he is trying to make the best film he can. In instances like *Heaven's Gate,* however, the director departed from the game plan he agreed to, as memorialized in the budget of the film, and proceeded with his own agenda. (For a useful account of the entire *Heaven's Gate* debacle, see Steven Bach's book, *Final Cut*.) All films represent a balance between the artistic and the financial, between the director's idealized vision and the reality of the budget. When the director signs the budget, he agrees to play by the rules of that particular game. To depart from those rules is to jeopardize your chances of doing films in the future.

A handful of directors have earned that rarest level of industry recognition, the right to exercise final cut on their pictures. Normally this right is reserved for the people that put up the money for the film—usually a motion picture studio. In practice, the studios work closely with the directors to arrive at a cut that satisfies both. Previews and invited audience research provide a database to assist in this process. The politics of the moment also play a role in determining how strongly a studio will assert itself.

Studios are very unlikely to step on the toes of an important director with whom they would like to work again. Hollywood is a very small town when it comes to matters such as this and no studio wants the reputation of running roughshod over the views of its directors. Sometimes the issue in dispute is the length of the film, sometimes the rating it has received from the M.P.A.A. (Motion Picture Association of America). At other times, anything from the score to the overall aesthetic of the film will be debated. It is always useful in such a dispute to know you have the last word, if matters come to that, and the studios will almost always back down.

What about independently made films? As difficult as it is today to get financing and distribution in place for an independent film, at least the filmmaker knows he will have greater artistic freedom than his studio-based colleagues enjoy. In most independent pictures, the financial backers are silent partners, or passive investors, in the project. This gives tremendous freedom to the director to work as he sees fit, without shaping his vision to accommodate the wishes of the studio executives. The comparatively few independent films that have gained wide acceptance in the marketplace indicate that artistic freedom does not always equate with commercial success.

The movie business has always provided an umbrella for filmmakers whose work is mainstream in nature, as well as those who tend to push the envelope out to new levels. Today, director

Steven Spielberg is prototypical of the director whose work is middle-of-the-road, although clearly done with flair and topspin so as to create films of tremendous worldwide appeal and popularity. Other directors, like Robert Altman, John Sayles, Alan Rudolph, or even the late Orson Welles, are representative of filmmakers whose tastes are more narrow gauge, and whose audiences tend to be more specialized. In the end, a director has to seek his own level and make those films that are most in sync with his own aesthetics and sensibilities. Obviously, the higher the budget, the larger the prospective audience has to be in order that the financial interests be made whole. This endless balancing of financial and creative interests underlies all of the economic structure of the picture business. It is always of critical concern to the director in search of financing for his pet project.

Much has been written recently about the opportunities afforded women and minorities to direct features. At this writing, it can be safely said that never have the chances been as good as they are today. The success of such films as *Big* and *Awakenings* propelled Penny Marshall to the front ranks of American directors. There is nothing like a smash commercial success to make studios suddenly look past the gender barrier in considering prospective directors for a film project. Parenthetically, it might be noted that the omission of Penny Marshall as a nominee for Best Director in the 1990 Academy Awards, although her film *Awakenings* was nominated for Best Picture and one of the two stars, Robert De Niro, was nominated for Best Actor, is considered an egregious, sexist slur by many industry observers. The omission was not a studio decision, but rather it was made by the members of the director's branch of the academy. Much the same slur was accorded director Barbra Streisand for *The Prince of Tides* a short time later. Statistics show that the opportunities for women to direct feature films, independents, and studio projects is only getting better. That there is some distance to go before anything approaching parity with men is achieved is an understatement.

Spike Lee has opened wide the door for promising black

directors today. The surprise success of *Boyz N the Hood* in the summer of 1991 has also helped demonstrate that black filmmakers now stand a better chance of getting their pictures made than at any other time in the history of cinema. There have always been a handful of black directors in the business, but today's opportunities, which coincide with the rise in black audience percentages and the greater sophistication on the part of film marketers in reaching black and crossover audiences, are unprecedented.

As the unquestioned captain of the creative ship in the making of a film, the director is the individual most aspirants to the film industry would like to become. There is no clear-cut course to follow to achieve this goal. Patience and persistence are certainly recommended skills to possess or develop. Talent and passion, probably in equal measure, are even more important in the attainment of the position of director. It is a widely held belief in the creative end of motion pictures that talent will out. That is, over time, talent—whether as an actor, a screenwriter, or a director—will be given its time at bat, its chance to express itself. Because of the competitive nature of the business, it is also necessary for the aspiring filmmaker to have a passion to make films, to see his work, his creative vision, reach the screen. Compromises may be necessary, but this is part of the game. When the costs are as great as they are in motion pictures, the creative process will usually be tempered by the demands of the financial interests. Arguably, it has always been this way in the arts dating back to the times when Michelangelo and other fine artists had to serve the interests of their patrons as well as respond to their own creative muses.

With many possibilities open to the aspiring director, and with the future appearing promising for the continued demand for feature films, there is reason for hope and optimism for the director beginning his career. In all likelihood, it will not be an easy road to travel, but both the financial and the personal rewards are immense. Some will succeed, so the best advice that can be given is to GO FOR IT!

SCREENWRITING

One of the country's great participant sports at this time is writing screenplays. In a recent poll in Los Angeles, California, passersby were stopped at random on a busy city street and asked how they were progressing with their screenplays. Remarkably, one out of three persons responded that they were doing very well with their screenwriting project.

Certainly, not all of these people will finish their screenplays, and an even smaller percentage will have their work considered in the professional marketplace. Still, one out of three people is a surprising, and perhaps alarming, statistic. The Writers Guild of America, West, the professional association to which virtually all professional screenwriters belong, has a service that allows writers to register their works. As will be seen, this establishes a time by which the screenplay was physically in existence. The guild is averaging in excess of 40,000 such registrations on an annual basis.

What is going on here? Why does America believe it can blithely turn out finished screenplays with comparative ease? The answer probably rests with several different propositions. First, a screenplay is much less intimidating to write than a novel. Between attending movies at the theaters, watching videocassettes, and even seeing theatrical features on television, millions of Americans are exposed to films. Many of these movies are so flawed or otherwise unsatisfactory that people are led into the seductive thought that they can do better. Instruction is readily available both in a formalized educational sense and through self-help means. After all, no boards or entrance exams need be passed to establish the writer's competence at his craft. Take the word processor, the typewriter, or even pencil and paper and go to work. Start writing a screenplay and magically you will have transformed yourself into a screenwriter.

But this is only the beginning of the process. The odds are prohibitively long that your work will find professional representation, i.e., by a literary agent, and longer still that it will ever sell or even be optioned. Having a picture made from your screenplay, while not as much of a long shot as winning a state lottery, occurs with only a select few.

Yet it happens. Screenplays are the lifeblood of the picture business. As Steven Spielberg said at a recent Academy Awards ceremony, "It all begins with the written word." Stars commit to scripts, as do directors, and ultimately studios. That studios are selective with what they buy is understandable. Somehow, among the hundreds of screenplays submitted to the studios weekly, quality shines through and the strong offerings get snapped up. It may take time, but it happens. Tom Schulman's successful script, *Dead Poets Society*, made the rounds for some years before commitments from Robin Williams and director Peter Weir converted a good writing sample into a studio film (which then became a hit). It happens.

To get to that point, a screenplay usually has to jump a series of hurdles at the studio. Initially, an agent or attorney must submit the script for the studio even to consider it. Unsolicited material will be returned in most cases without being read. This policy is to stave off litigation by nonprofessional writers who historically have insisted that their ideas were "stolen" by the studio. If the studio elects to consider a project, it will customarily give the script to a reader whose job is to synopsize it in a page to a page and a half, and then add a half-page of personal recommendation. If the reader is unimpressed, the script will be rejected without further consideration. The sheer volume of material submitted to the studios makes a system of reader coverage necessary in the industry.

Should the reader endorse a screenplay, it will generally be read by one or more production executives whose responsibility it is to keep promising projects in the pipeline at all times. Different studios will be looking for different projects (or staying away from them) all the time. If a certain screenplay clicks with the decision makers of the moment, the studio will endeavor to cut a deal with the writer's representative. This process will involve another team of players from the business affairs or the legal departments. New hurdles must be overcome at this time if the deal is to be consummated and the screenplay acquired or optioned by the studio.

The process is virtually the same if the screenplay is submitted directly to a producer or director. The only real difference is that the producer or director (or even the actor) will usually have less money to spend than the studio.

Recent years have seen staggering breakthroughs in the amount of money that a screenplay can command. The Writers Guild sets minimum payments for high-and low-budget motion pictures. It uses a budget amount of $2.5 million as the breakpoint for low- and high-budget films. At present, the minimum amount owed for the purchase of a screenplay without a treatment is approximately $18,500 for a low-budget film and approximately $38,000 for a high-budget film. These amounts are applicable only to guild contracts, or those writers employed by a guild signatory. This includes all of the major film studios.

The upper end of the register is the one that has seen the most movement of late. In 1989 and 1990, the marketplace was defined by vast sums that were paid for "spec" scripts, or those scripts written on speculation, without a buyer commissioning them. Why the sudden increase in the value of spec scripts? That question is still being debated. In part, it grew out of the uncertainties of the market, or more appropriately, the shifting tastes of film-going audiences. In part, overall budgets were rising dramatically and screenplay prices accompanied this phenomenon. Also, Hollywood has long been a town with a thinly disguised lemming quality. Let someone else want something or somebody, and suddenly everyone wants it. This is often characterized as "heat" in industry parlance. Frequently, there is nothing of any substance to support such rapid escalations in price or value—only the fact that something or someone has abruptly become very fashionable.

Whatever the reason, in this period the prices for scripts rose to $1.5 million, then $2 million, and finally reached the reported $3 million received by Joe Eszterhas for his screenplay *Basic Instinct.* Perhaps inevitably, prices began to fall shortly thereafter. Led by a well-circulated "internal" memorandum written by Walt Disney Chairman Jeff Katzenberg in early 1991, his company (and by inference the entire picture industry) was taken to task for spending vast sums of money on screenplays developed outside the studio auspices, i.e., spec scripts. He lamented "a tidal wave of runaway costs and mindless competition" that was hitting Hollywood. He urged a return to betting on talent, talent able to formulate exciting ideas and translate them into compelling stories. The circulation of this memorandum coincided with a falloff in the prices garnered by spec scripts. Studios suddenly became more cautious and agents described the market as one filled with uncertainty. With all of this supposed retrenchment, a $1 million price tag on a screenplay is far from unusual today.

As the business has ebbed and flowed, screenwriters have been greatly assisted by their guild, the Writers Guild of America, East, and the Writers Guild of America, West. Much like the Directors Guild of America in terms of services and protections it has secured for its membership, the W.G.A. has negotiated such matters as minimum compensation, pension and welfare benefits, residuals, and health benefits. Jurisdictionally, the guild uses the Mississippi River to divide the country into East and West. The respective guild headquarters are as follows:

The Writers Guild of America, East, Inc.
555 West 57th Street
New York, New York 10019

The Writers Guild of America, West, Inc.
8955 Beverly Boulevard
West Hollywood, California 90048

Among the services available to the membership are furnishing copies of minimum basic agreements, publishing newsletters, providing help in finding an agent, and registering material so as to provide the writer with a specific date when it can be established that his material was in existence. Membership is available to any person who has been employed as a writer or has sold original material in the screen, television, or radio media.

It is understandable if the beginning writer wonders what those persons who buy screenplays have in mind. What are they looking for as they wade through the hundreds upon hundreds of scripts that reach their desks? In the most fundamental terms, as Jeff Katzenberg suggests, they are looking for a good story. Ideally, the script will be populated with interesting and compelling characters, but more than anything, it needs to be a good story. The further along the story is, in terms of being successfully worked out, the better. Conversely, the more the story represents a good idea in search of details and good characters, the less appeal it will have.

For a while in the late 1980s, the industry was preoccupied with "high-concept" scripts. Essentially a television notion brought over to feature films, the high-concept script is one that tells well in less than a minute. In other words, it is a screenplay that can be comfortably presented in two sentences as in a *TV Guide* listing. There are endless examples from this period. "A high-powered mogul falls in love with a Los Angeles prostitute." (*Pretty Woman*). "Terrorists seize a modern skyscraper only to discover that they have inadvertently also entrapped a tough police officer" (*Die Hard*). "Two unlikely police buddies and partners, one black and one white, do battle against the bad guys while also managing to have a helluva time" (*Lethal Weapon*).

High concepts and high-concept salesmanship reached a peak when the film version of the television series "Dragnet" was reportedly sold by the producer pitching only the familiar theme, "Dum-de-dum-dum."

In time, it was demonstrated at the box office that the high-concept notion is not a panacea, but only one kind of film that may enjoy audience success. Hugely successful films like *Rain Man* or *Dead Poets Society* were certainly not high concept in nature. The public has very catholic tastes in motion pictures. Undoubtedly, many film-goers would prefer their films to achieve some degree of excellence, or present some breakthrough in technique or story. But many others pay their money for simple, mindless entertainment. The film can be funny, scary, sexy, thrilling, silly, romantic—virtually anything. If it "works" for audiences, people will find it and see it, often more than once. From the standpoint of the writer who is involved in the creation of the story, the beginning of the process, this means wrapping his talent in a totally professional package.

The submission of screenplays is, in part, a process that defeats the old saw that you can't tell a book by its cover. If a screenplay is not written in the professionally accepted style, it will be rejected without further consideration. Numerous books detail what is meant by a professional screenplay format. This means that the script should be no more than 130 pages and no less than 100 pages in length. Screenplays average 120 pages, with the popular convention holding that each page is equal to one minute of screen time. Margins should be set along customary lines, and other popular conventions should be observed. It is a mistake to punctuate the script with artwork, long speeches, camera directions (unless absolutely necessary for the scene), lists of characters, and the like. All of these ingredients brand the writer as a nonprofessional and lead to the rejection of his submission, often without further attention.

It does little good to rail against the system that rejects creative product by appearance alone. Experience over many years has convinced Hollywood that it is far better to stick with the professionals, even if there is the one in a million chance that something of worth will be discarded along with all of the chaff. It makes great sense, therefore, to respond to the marketplace by learning the proper screenplay format and utilizing it in your submission. Not everything is etched in stone in a manner that permits no flexibility or creative expression. But the basic format is a generally accepted one and should be followed.

The beginning screenwriter should do the job of the writer and not step on the toes of the director, the cameraman, or even the production manager. Thus, it is the job of the director, not the screenwriter, to call for given camera angles. Similarly, unless needed for plot purposes, it is the director's job to decide on the music cues, special effects and other such considerations. If someday you direct a film, that is the time to assert yourself in these areas—not when you are writing a screenplay. The numbering of scenes is the task of the production manager, not the screenwriter. It never hurts to be cognizant of the cost of what you put down on paper, but that too is not your worry. Stick to the story and the characters—and be certain that you have put them in the proper form.

Help is available on this front. Among the better books for those who would instruct themselves are:

Dmytryk, Edward. *On Screen Writing*. Boston: Focal, 1985.

Field, Syd. *Screenplay*. New York: Dell, 1982.

King, Viki. *How to Write a Movie in 21 Days*. New York: Harper & Row, 1988.

Seger, Linda. *Creating Unforgettable Characters*. New York: Holt, 1990.

Many colleges and universities, as well as adult education centers and a variety of other educational facilities, offer beginning and advanced screenwriting courses. It is, after all, not an equipment-intensive discipline, and it can therefore be offered by many resources at comparatively little expense. In addition to complete courses, there are many weekend seminars offered by such groups as the American Film Institute (AFI) as well as other more entrepreneurial sorts, all of whom can provide valuable points of departure for the beginning writer.

In the final analysis, screenwriting is not totally dissimilar to learning the rudiments of playing a musical instrument or applying paint to a canvas. Everyone wants to know at the outset if he has talent—or if he is wasting his time. No one is smart enough to know the answer to this question. In art or music, the artist must learn his craft before anyone can make a determination about his artistry. To get to that level takes dedication and commitment. Then, and only then, will it be possible to make judgments about the individual's talent. And even then, reasonable people may come down on opposite sides of that critical question.

In screenwriting, there are no shortcuts to developing one's craft. Learning the form and developing the skills necessary to commit one's ideas to paper are requisite beginnings. Thereafter, such intangibles as talent, dedication, perseverance, and the like will inevitably factor into the equation. The dedicated writer keeps writing, each screenplay bringing his craft to a new level, each rewrite elevating his work to a higher degree of accomplishment.

Then what? Once you have saved in your word processor something you sincerely believe to be a great screenplay, what do you do? Unfortunately, the answer to that question invites more questions than it answers. Find an agent. Most reputable buyers will look at a screenplay only if it is submitted by an attorney or an agent. Over the years, unsolicited submissions, which has come to mean submissions that do not come from recognizable agents or attorneys, have spawned more lawsuits than they have produced viable movie packages. In self-protection, the studios and reputable producers have slammed the door shut on most unsolicited submissions. So how do you get an agent? Again, the $64,000 question.

The Writers Guild will provide, to members and nonmembers alike, lists of agents who will look at unsolicited material. They recommend that your material be accompanied by a stamped, self-addressed envelope; and they warn you that often you will never hear from the agent again. While agents are located all over the country, the majority of useful agents—at least those who can do the beginning screenwriter some good—are found in New York or Los Angeles. Most are literary agents, and not talent agents. This is often the difference between those agents who represent writers and directors, the literary agent, and those agents who represent performing talent, the so-called talent agent. These distinctions often blur, and it is difficult to separate one agent from another. Certainly, the names of agents supplied by the Writers Guild are a place to begin. But it may not provide all the answers.

As a general rule, it is *never* advisable to give an agent a fee to read your screenplay. No agent franchised by the Writers Guild of America is permitted to charge such a reading fee. Indeed, no agent should ever be given fees to represent your work. The agent takes a percentage of the moneys you earn. He should not be paid anything in advance, even if it is disguised as a reading fee or a literary service fee. This is the hallmark of an unscrupulous or unethical operator. No matter how desperate the screenwriter becomes, or how seductive or persuasive the agent sounds, never send him money for examining or evaluating your work. Without exception, such payment will be thrown to the winds, and not spent in the furtherance of your best interests.

While it may be very frustrating to wait for some word from an agent, knowing that the agent is not a buyer but only a step along the way, virtually every writer has had to suffer through the same thing. The early stages of a writing career are very difficult—just as they are for acting and other artistic endeavors. The writer should keep writing and keep trying to scratch some kind of toehold in the business.

The early stages of seeking an agent and getting the lay of the land should, in all probability, be accomplished in Los Angeles. For most people, this is a significant career step, entailing a move to an expensive and quite intimidating town. Certainly you can hedge this somewhat by submitting scripts by mail and trying to do business by telephone and fax. The task of launching a career from out of town, however, is much more difficult. The movie business is Hollywood-based. Once established, like William Goldman, for example, you can live anywhere and simply travel to Los Angeles periodically for meetings. The unknown writer, however, does himself a major disservice by not being at the scene of the action. Those all-important first breaks can arise in altogether unpredictable and serendipitous ways, but almost never in Nebraska, Kansas, or Alabama.

What is the best example of your work to show? Again, you should be the judge, and there is no right answer. Most agents will ask you to select one piece of material from your portfolio. It should showcase what you do best. Comedy, action-adventure, romance—select an example of your strongest work. Even if the script is under option, it may serve you well as a writing sample. As such it can get you representation as well as writing assignments. It should always be kept in mind that at any given moment in Los Angeles there are many writing assignments available to writers in all price ranges. Thus, a new screenwriter, if on the scene and represented by an aggressive agent, may have his writing sample read, be invited to a meeting, and with luck, come away with a plum assignment. It could be an adaptation, a rewrite, or the development of someone's original idea. These are opportunities that the professional writer covets, chances to earn a living at his craft.

Once an agent takes on a writer as a client, the agent receives a commission of 10 percent of all sums the writer receives. This is the guild maximum and it attaches to 10 percent of the writer's gross income. Generally, the agent gets his commission whether the job was unearthed by the writer or by the agent. Many new writers are represented without signed papers. In the early stages of their careers, agents may represent them on a trial basis only. Obviously this is less helpful than a signed commitment, but it may be all that is available. In this regard, most new writers recognize the need to light fires under their agents continually. Hollywood moves very much by pressure and by maintaining an active presence. As the old saying goes, "Out of sight, out of mind." While it would be nice for a writer to have an enthusiastic agent represent him above all his other clients, things don't work that way. Even with an agent handling a screenwriter's career, the writer will have to network and make new connections wherever possible, both professionally and socially. Some of this becomes easier for an established writer, but these tasks never disappear completely from the screenwriter's life.

As experience grows, often with coaching by an agent, writers will develop expertise in the skill of "giving good meetings." They will learn how to "pitch" their ideas to a buyer, how to be flexible and resilient in the face of criticism, and how to roll with the inevitable punches. The better the writer is at the verbal gymnastics involved in pitch meetings, the better his chances of landing jobs. Certainly his writing skills are of preeminent importance, but the skills involved in meetings and pitches should never be underestimated.

The business of the movie business, whether one is an actor, a director, or a screenwriter, is often about choices. The beginning artist has very few choices. He takes what he can, hopes to earn a living, or at least to survive, and hopes for better times. With some success, the opportunity to pick and choose among different opportunities presents itself. Maybe at this point the writer undertakes a speculative script by choice. Maybe the book he always wanted to adapt suddenly becomes available. The good agent is as adept at career guidance at this stage as he should be at finding employment and negotiating deals. He becomes an important sounding board for the writer in keeping his career moving in the right direction, not to mention preserving the integrity of the writer in his work.

Many new writers labor under the misconception that the world lies in wait to steal their ideas, treatments, and even screenplays. Nothing could be further from the truth. In fact, this kind of paranoia is more the mark of the amateur than anything else connected with the writing business. Legitimate buyers, studios, and reputable producers are not in the business of stealing literary creations. Quite the opposite. They take pains to try not to put themselves in the position of even appearing to be misappropriating literary product. You can protect your material by securing a copyright, registering it with the Writers Guild of America, or sending it to yourself by registered mail and not opening the envelope. Such protection does make prudent business sense. You establish that on a certain date your material was in existence. Note that it in no way provides any assurance as to its originality, as a patent does for an invention.

On occasion, there are exceptions to the notion that studios do not misappropriate writers' work. In the celebrated case in 1990 where writer Art Buchwald and his producer, Alain Bernheim, successfully sued Paramount Pictures Corporation for taking the story that was to become the Eddie Murphy movie *Coming to America,* there were other factors that influenced Paramount's conduct. In any event, that case is very much the exception to the standards of ethical behavior that exist in the industry as regards screenplays and other forms of literary material.

Where the beginning writer needs to pay very close attention, however, is in dealing with nonsignatory fly-by-night producers. The real danger here is that he is going to do the work and not get paid. The best approach to getting whatever money is due under the operative agreement is to withhold delivery of the script until the producer hands over the payment for it. Once the writer has parted with his script, he is relying on the good faith of the producer—and that may not be there. It is always helpful to use an attorney when a deal is being negotiated. Business is business, and the beginning writer may not have the support team of agents and attorneys standing by to protect him on the negotiation of his deal. Seek out an entertainment attorney to review the papers. The expense involved has proved its value many, many times.

Attorneys may also play an important role in clarifying what the writer can write about without obtaining releases or other rights. Issues regarding public domain and copyright questions can be both technical and determinative of what the writer should spend his time working on. If the rights to a property are already held, it is but an exercise to labor over a screenplay adaptation of it in the hope that something good might happen. There is the further question of when rights must be secured from a living person in order to write about him. The law in this sensitive area is in flux, and the opinion of a qualified attorney should be sought early in the project's life. Beware of bringing such matters to the family retainer, the good old lawyer friend of your parents who has drawn up wills and closed real estate deals. Entertainment practice is a highly specialized branch of the law, one that requires much knowledge of current business practices as well as current statutory or case law.

When the skills to write a screenplay have been assimilated, and when sufficient time has been logged in writing projects, most writers must face the ultimate question of whether writing is truly for them. It has many more lonely, anxious hours than it has hours filled with glamour and excitement. It certainly has more time of frustration than it has moments of triumph. So how do you know if writing is your calling? On what basis can one reasonably conclude that a writing career is the correct choice for his life? Novelist-screenwriter (and director) Michael Crichton once said to me that he had to write—that the words were in him and had to have a means of getting out. I suspect that most writers feel the same way. They may resent the seclusion, the hard work, the times when answers elude them, but most wouldn't trade their lives for what might appear less problem-filled or outwardly more seductive.

Working screenwriters keep different schedules and adapt working times to their own life-styles. Some write compulsively during all their waking hours. Others keep to rigid schedules of writing for a prescribed length of time each day, editing for another period, and conducting the rest of their lives in the remaining time. Some writers stay up with the latest in word-processing equipment; some swear by their old typewriters; and others continue to write by hand on yellow legal pads. Clearly, it is not the tools of the trade that spell success. It is, rather, the words that are written that contain the magic.

During what may be a dry spell financially, when the new writer is trying to get established, there are some things that might be kept in mind. First and foremost, keep writing. Doing so has proved for many to be the strongest link to sanity that the writer has. Your craft will improve, your passion will be kept at a high level, and you just may turn out something that is both worthwhile and salable. For many, the problem is not so much continuing to write as it is providing some money for sustenance. Many writers have successfully found employment as a reader during this period of their lives. Some studios have union readers and don't take on free-lance readers. Others, as well as many agencies and producers, hire free-lance readers to cover material for them and turn in their synopses and recommendations. This may be an ideal job for the aspiring writer for several reasons. It is a cottage industry that can be performed at home, at hours of the writer's selection. It also exposes the writer to what other writers are writing about and even thinking about. Finally, it offers the opportunity for some professional discourse, which could prove beneficial to the writer's career in a variety of ways. Depending on the employer, reading could pay from $50 to $75 for a screenplay, to considerably more for a novel. Usually, prospective readers are auditioned by story editors and given sample screenplays to cover. There is considerable movement in the reader's position as readers move on to other callings, and it can be very fruitful for the newly arrived screenwriter to pursue.

It should always be kept in mind that the business is bigger than just the studios. Cable companies, television companies, and suppliers to motion pictures, cable, and network television all deal in material and therefore require everything from scripts to readers.

What advice can be given to steer a writer toward some particular subject matter or genre? Probably nothing of any value. Some argue that people should write about what they know. Others insist that this body of information is probably too dull to exploit and that the writer is better advised to use his imagination and concoct wonderful and fanciful characters and stories. On balance, the writer is best off writing about that which affects him strongly. There are certainly many writers who can perform their writing skills with fine, mechanical dexterity and don't have to have any emotional involvement in their work. Most writers work differently. They write at their best when they are deeply concerned with what they are writing. These passions lead them in wholly unpredictable directions, directions that are often as surprising to them as to anyone else. No one can predict which film subjects will prove popular with audiences, or which are the subjects that aspiring writers should essay. There are many too many "unlikely" hit films to draw conclusions of this kind.

Successful writer William Goldman once observed of Hollywood that "nobody knows anything." This is a good notion to keep in mind. It is tempting to try to write clones of the successful films in the marketplace. This is an error. Write what you want to write, and let everything else fall into place. The product you turn out will be better, more representative of who you are and what you are capable of delivering. Otherwise, your work will be derivative and below your potential. If you have chosen to write in a familiar genre, that is not necessarily a mistake. Be certain as you set about obliging the various conventions of your genre that you infuse the plot with a freshness and the characters with some depth and an element of surprise that gives the finished material a sense of singularity, of originality. The best films of Steven Spielberg, for example, always seem to incorporate familiar elements, but are presented with topspin, with handling that makes them appear altogether fresh and new.

Objectively speaking, it may be harder to get a character piece produced than a strong plot-driven narrative. Good character dramas often depend solely on casting if they are to succeed in the marketplace. A film like *Rain Man* would have been far less likely to score as well as it did at the box office, director Barry Levinson notwithstanding, were it not for the casting of Dustin Hoffman and Tom Cruise. Yet if that special character is rattling around your head, write about him. Don't get shaped by the thinking of the guys in suits. Look inward to what is driving you.

Momentum or heat is only as far away as a successful film. One popular magazine that covers motion pictures refers to writers enjoying sudden, and very profitable, popularity as "Flavors of the Month." If celebrity envelops you in that manner, you can literally go from being destitute to being a millionaire overnight. Your writing price, which may not have even existed moments before, may now reach well into six figures. You will have your choice of assignments, job offers, and all of the emoluments that an industry can shower upon you. One young, hot writer, still in his mid-twenties, seemed astounded when he was offered $100,000 a week to do a hurried rewrite on a studio picture. This is the time when a good agent can earn his keep. Not only can he maximize the economics of the deals, but probably more importantly, he can judge the prevailing winds so that the fire of popularity is not blown out. The young writer can look to a long and successful career in the business. It is a great error to mess it up by not responding to success as one should.

A final notion the beginning screenwriter should be aware

of is that he is not alone. There are many other writers at work who experience the same frustrations and breakthroughs. It will often prove very beneficial to stay in touch with them. Advice on everything from software systems to curing writer's block can always be gotten from one's peers. They meet informally. They communicate through the W.G.A. newsletter. They are in touch electronically through bulletin boards and modems. The Writers Guild of America, West, since installing its bulletin board in 1988, has logged in calls from almost half of its approximately 7,000 members. These electronic forums can give assistance in research, provide current information, or simply allow for the venting of frustrations. They are there and available—at all hours. It is too valuable a resource for the writer not to use.

If screenwriting holds any appeal for the individual casting a yearning look at the motion picture industry, then start writing. Have something to say, and say it in a manner and with a format that gives your words the appearance of being professionally written. Separate yourself from the amateurs who haven't taken the time to learn to write a screenplay properly. Remember, you are a writer if you write, not if you have an agent, or sell a work, or have a script produced. Writers write. Stop thinking about it, if that's what you want to do, and do it!

ACTING

Times have most assuredly changed in Hollywood. Schwab's Drug Store, scene of some real and many mythical "discoveries" of actors, no longer exists on Sunset Boulevard. But the hopes and dreams of many wannabe actors remain alive.

One noted casting director for motion pictures, Mike Fenton, likes to recount the famous story about the unknown actor walking on a studio lot. Turning the corner in one direction, she encounters a film director. He stops her and excitedly asks if she is an actress. Discovering that she is, he casts her on the spot for his current film and instructs her to get in touch with his casting director right away to set the deal. Had she turned the corner in the opposite direction, quips Fenton, she would have been run down by a fast-moving truck. Is it all determined only by chance? Is success or failure as an actor purely a matter of serendipity?

Certainly luck plays a role. It does in most other pursuits as well. But there are always ways for a person to make his own luck. There is information that may be gathered, preparations that can be made, and courses of action that, if followed, should improve one's chances for success as an actor in the motion picture business.

Initially, it is difficult not to be somewhat deterred by odds that appear prohibitive. Of the more than 70,000 actors who are members of the Screen Actors Guild (SAG), it is estimated that but 3,000 of them earn a living from acting each year. Eliminating for the moment commercials, the theater, television, and other acting opportunities, and looking only at theatrical feature films, this figure becomes quite comprehensible. There may be 350 theatrical films produced every year. Each averages twenty-four acting parts. Of course, many of the same actors will act in more than one of these films. Just looking at the arithmetic may be enough to discourage the star-struck aspiring actor. Many agents and casting directors will further discourage aspiring actors by recounting for their benefit the difficulties in achieving stardom, and the overwhelming number of setbacks that will be experienced along the way. As in so many areas of the motion picture industry, all of these words of pessimism and discouragement tend to fall on deaf ears. If an aspiring actor possesses the drive and the persistence, coupled with certain fundamental skills, he won't take no for an answer.

If you are asking yourself if you should gear up and take a stab at an acting career, there are certain considerations to keep in mind. If your motivation is clear, or even confused, what attributes should you possess to go forward in this highly competitive area? Few would argue that the key ingredient for success in this field is talent. There are certainly many definitions of talent, and nowhere is this more evident than in movies. There is a world of difference between the late Sir Laurence Olivier and, say, Clint Eastwood. Yet both have been very successful as leading men. Or between Meryl Streep and Debra Winger; or Paul Newman and Burt Reynolds. Yet, they all share that same common denominator—talent.

Unlike in almost every other field except modeling, special attention is also given to the package in which the talent comes wrapped. What kind of looks do you possess? What "type" are you and how distinctive an image do you present? Actors come in all shapes and sizes, and it is wrong to write yourself off if you do not resemble a classic description of good looks. The ability to project a unique representation as called for by the role and shaped by the director, is what matters. Types are certainly important, but more than ever before, people today are casting against type. In cliché terms, this is often conveyed by suggesting that you never get a prostitute to play a prostitute. Casting against type will produce a more interesting performance.

Training and experience are also vital parts of the success equation in Hollywood. There are certainly numerous instances of actors who learned their craft on the job and had no prior experience or training. Many more have worked long and hard to perfect their skills. They have studied, often with more than one coach, performed wherever they could—from neighborhood playhouses to student films—and kept after the acting business all day, every day. As with many things in life, if you want it enough, you owe it to yourself to do your best. For almost everyone, that means putting in the hours of work and study to try to accomplish the ends you seek.

Along the way, you will acquire another critical ingredient in the mix—professionalism. Nothing is valued more highly on a movie set than professionalism. Conversely, unprofessional behavior on a set comes close to being the cardinal sin of moviemaking. With films today costing in excess of $28 million, there is no faster way to find yourself out of the business than to develop a reputation for being unprofessional. This could result from drugs or alcohol, not knowing your lines, creating a scene with the director, or any of a number of other excesses. The limits of what constitutes professional behavior are learned by experience and are important always to be kept in mind.

Andrea Eastman is a talent agent working for International Creative Management (ICM). She has worked as an agent and a personal manager for actors throughout her professional career. She has also been involved in the casting process and received a casting credit for *The Godfather.* Eastman assesses the promise of a young actor by looking at a number of qualities. First and foremost, for her, is what she terms the actor's "presence." She describes this in terms of whatever makes that actor "special." It might be an impish sense of humor, an overpowering sexuality, a sense of danger lurking beneath the surface, or a strong likability. If you reflect on movie stars who have demonstrated some degree of staying power, who have remained stars even when they are not in the theaters with a hot movie, you will note that they possess many different qualities. Indeed, the wide diversity of types and personalties strongly suggests that it is less a formula for stardom, and more the unique aspects of the individual that allow for a rise to the top.

Eastman doesn't pretend to focus the equivalent of the eye of the camera on prospective clients. With few exceptions, she is not at all certain when the camera will "love" her client as it did, for example, the late Marilyn Monroe. Instead, Eastman tries to identify what she calls "star quality." Again, she is looking for a presence to go along with acting skills and a marketable look. The actor's talent, she feels, is something of a given. Once in a great while an actor or actress of exceptional talent bursts onto the scene. More often, someone arrives with a special quality, some aspect of their look or personality that leaves a lasting impression. That impression is made originally with casting directors, agents, producers, and directors, and ultimately with audiences. While elusive of precise definition, it is, in the words of the cliché, something that people recognize when they see it.

The professionals in this business are quick to point out that it is not only the attributes the actor comes by naturally but also the skills he has acquired by hard work that ensure success. Much as in the world of professional sports, many have the physical skills, but not everyone will make it. There are more parts to the equation. Certainly there is a luck factor that accompanies this career, as it does so many others. Persistence and the ability to overcome the hurdles that will almost certainly be present are other qualities that the successful actor must have. Out of the ranks of many, few are chosen. Of the few that make it, most work hard to make choices go in their favor.

An actor who enjoyed the best of reputations for his motion picture work, Spencer Tracy, once said, "There is nothing more to acting than learning your lines and remembering not to bump into the furniture." For most actors, however, there is much more to think about.

Much has been written about "types" that go on to become

stars in the movie business. For many years, the classic leading men tended to conform to certain basic physical types. Other actors fell into other categories, from character leads to novelty acts to musical performers. In a sense, director Mike Nichols's choice of Dustin Hoffman to play the lead in *The Graduate* in the late 1960s proved a liberating one for many, many actors. Never again would the notion of who was a leading man and who wasn't be defined as narrowly as it had been. Nichols went with acting ability, and the results were profound. To be sure, such actors as Spencer Tracy and Paul Muni had always enjoyed reputations both as fine actors and as movie stars. Yet they were certainly in the minority. After *The Graduate,* the door to play leads was opened much wider, to the obvious delight of the acting community.

Should you enter these sweepstakes? Do you think you have what it takes to carve a niche for yourself in the motion picture business? Are you possessed of the right stuff to make it as an actor in today's Hollywood? Of course, these are questions that only *you* can answer at the present time. It is clear that new talent is being "discovered" every day. Newcomers are getting work, careers are being built, stars are being made. It is a continual process, and the best person to judge whether you should get into this race is you, yourself.

If you decide to give it a shot, there are some tools that should be assembled to facilitate giving yourself a fair chance at making it in Hollywood. First off, you had better be certain you have a telephone. In addition, you will need an answering service, or at least an answering machine from which you can always pick up your messages. The telephone is your umbilical cord to the industry, your source of news about life-sustaining employment. Leads, callbacks, even offers of employment come at all hours, and it is imperative that you have ready access to this information. Since many, if not most, beginning actors supplement their incomes through other employment opportunities, such as waiting on tables, driving limousines or teaching aerobics, it is essential to stay connected by means of the phone.

The aspiring actor will also need pictures and a résumé that can be left with prospective employers. As with all of Hollywood, while there may be an outwardly relaxed air about all of this, there is a clear-cut underlying need for professionalism. If the pictures or the résumé appear amateurish, that alone will brand the actor as unemployable. Pictures should be eight inches by ten inches, in black and white. Color is a waste of money, and even frowned upon by most casting people. Head shots or a composite, or both, should be shot professionally by any of a number of professional services and should be developed with a glossy finish. Usually, a well-prepared résumé is affixed to the back of the photograph so that interested parties can conveniently recall who the actor is and what experience he has had. Many actors take the extra step of having their names printed on the bottom of the photograph. Touches like this never hurt. Anything that is seen as professional in quality and that helps prospective employers single you out furthers you in the right direction.

It is a sad commentary on how misguided some would-be actors can be, and the cruel treatment that lies in store for them, when one learns about responses to unsolicited pictures and résumés. In my days as a talent agent, every mail delivery seemed to contain pictures and letters from actor wannabes. Some agents dutifully maintained private collections of these pictures, which they referred to as their "dog files." Snapshots mounted on shirt boards, letters with lipstick kisses, Polaroid pictures in provocative poses—these and many other like submissions would arrive with alarming frequency. In a word, if you decide to try for an acting career, do it the right way. It is hard enough to make it in any event; there is no point at all in further complicating the process by proceeding in the wrong way.

If you possess a videotape, on ½ or ¾ inch, of your performances, it is never a bad idea to have the tape available for viewing. Clearly it is better if your clips come from feature films or television programs. If they are derived from amateur theatrical productions, you have to decide how professional your performance appears and how professional the overall quality of the tape presentation really is. It is better not to show tape than to show tape that has the unmistakable aura of amateurism surrounding it.

When professional pictures have been prepared, you will probably want one or two shots to be printed in the "Academy Players Directory." This publication, with three editions per year, costs $20 per edition and offers the reader a visual reference for names and faces. To get listed, you need only bring your photographs to the Academy of Arts and Sciences Building at 8949 Wilshire Boulevard, Los Angeles, California. You will be asked to select the appropriate category you want to be listed under (Young Leading Man/Lady, Leading Man/Lady, etc.) and provide information about your agent and his telephone number. You don't need an agent to have your pictures included, and many actors list their own telephone number, or that of their service. For the actor beginning his career, an entry in this directory is indispensable.

Presumably, if you have your sights set on the movie business, you have seen fit to locate yourself near Los Angeles. Sure, there are some parts to be had in New York, or Miami, or Orlando, or Chicago—but not many. Again, the odds are tough enough already. There is no reason to make them tougher. If you have relocated to Los Angeles, the cost of living will instantly pose a significant problem. So too will the need for an automobile. L.A. is a big, sprawling city, and the studios are located all around it. To be able to get where you need to go, on a timely basis, you must have a car.

Up-to-date information about the business is another useful and necessary tool for the aspiring actor. Although not written primarily for actors, the "trade papers," *Daily Variety* and *The Hollywood Reporter*, are considered necessary reading by most industry personnel. Available by subscription or at newsstands all over town, the trades are often read before the daily newspaper by those trying to keep up with the ever-changing motion picture landscape.

Other sources of information exist as well. Two bookstores, among many, have proved particularly useful for those seeking current and classic material on acting and the movie industry. They are:

Larry Edmunds Cinema and Theatre Book Shop
6658 Hollywood Boulevard
Hollywood, California
(213) 463-3273

Samuel French, Inc.
7623 Sunset Boulevard
Hollywood, California
(213) 876-0570

Hollywood is a town rife with gossip. In many respects, gossip fuels the town and propels it forward from day to day. As with all such talk, some of it is true, and some of it is wholly apocryphal. Information that the aspiring actor receives usually has to be followed up in some way if only to verify the story. Information will come from the trades, from networking with friends, from a host of sources. Inevitably, some leads will turn out to be dead ends, but some will bear fruit. Resign yourself to the inevitable wild goose chases, and continue to seek out information wherever you can find it, and then act upon it.

When the aspiring actor seeks tools to facilitate his succeeding in motion pictures, perhaps the most important one is the agent. An agent actively pursues work for his clients, negotiates the terms of employment, and provides career guidance to continually evolve a strategy for moving up the ladder of recognition to better and better parts and more and more choices. If all of this seems beyond the reasonable expectation of the beginning actor, take comfort in the fact that most actors have had to start without an agent in exactly the same predicament. There are more than 300 agencies in Los Angeles. The three largest, ICM, the William Morris Agency, and CAA, are all but out of reach for the beginning actor. Their overhead costs are simply too overwhelming for them to spend time nurturing the careers of aspiring actors. They seek out established performers, those capable of immediately being sold for motion pictures and television.

There are, however, many smaller agencies that represent actors. A newcomer's best chance for representation lies with agencies of this kind. Always avoid those few unscrupulous agents who ask for some kind of fee from you to cover their initial "expenses" involved in representing you. Such agents do not hold a franchise from the Screen Actors Guild—always a good thing to verify before signing a representation agreement—and are usually fly-by-night operators who prey on the unsuspecting. An honest, hardworking agent will have an information flow far beyond any that you are able to develop for yourself. It is his follow-through on this information that will finally secure employment for you.

Would that there were an easy answer to the question of how one obtains an agent. Doing so requires making rounds, utilizing any and all connections one has, and most of all, persistence. A call from a producer or a director to an agent, made on your behalf, is an excellent way to capture the interest of the agent. Especially at the early stages of a career, aggressively selling oneself is a necessary part of the process of getting ahead. If you can get an agent to meet you, or even better, to see your work, you will at least have gotten a time at bat. If things don't work out now, for whatever reason, they might at some time in the future. The more meetings and contacts you establish, the better you serve your career.

The agent is in business. He commissions your gross income (to the tune of 10 percent regardless of who turns up the job). Under SAG rules, a client can leave an agency, regardless of the term of the agreement, if no work has been offered to the client for ninety consecutive days. Thus, the agent who signs you must be prepared to go out and work for you. Smaller agents are accustomed to taking on new clients and endeavoring to build their careers. As progress is made, the money you earn will become greater, and so too will the amounts the agent earns. Most actors are represented by different agents, at different companies, at various times in their professional careers. There are myriad reasons why actors seek other representation—some good and some not. Bad career advice, losing out on a job to another client of the same agency, inaccessibility of the agent, unsatisfactory deal terms—these and many other reasons cause actors to change agents. At the highest levels of the profession, the superstar actors find that the only logical reason to pay an agent the 10 percent commission he requires (rather than paying a lawyer by the hour to negotiate deals) is to gain access to material and other creative elements that the agency will combine into motion picture packages. This could account for today's concentration of major stars at CAA. The inherent risk in the setup is that sometimes big stars are attracted by a megapersonality agent, only to discover that they rarely have contact with that agent once they sign agency papers.

Casting directors are the other category of professional that the new actor must get to know. You must meet as many as possible, try whenever you work theatrically to get casting directors to attend, and in general become known by the members of this important segment of the community. The casting director is in a constant dialogue with producers and directors, with agents, and with talent. Since casting directors are involved in casting every movie made, it is important to create a favorable impression on them.

As with other aspects of a newcomer's career, the more aggressively the actor "works" this end of the business, the better the results he can expect. Some carry themselves better at these kinds of interviews, but every actor should do what he can to learn to convert such opportunities into successes that will ultimately produce work.

Success at an interview, whether with a casting director, an agent, or a filmmaker, is something that the actor too frequently leaves to chance. To be sure, you may be the wrong type and not get the part for that reason alone. Next to modeling, there are very few other jobs in which the physical look is as important as it is in acting. The impression the actor leaves, however, even if he is unsuccessful in landing that part, can result in offers at a later time.

The interview is definitely not a meeting of equals. It is more akin to a sales encounter with one person selling and the other making up his mind whether or not to buy. This inequality has given rise to the stories, real and mythical, of the casting couch sexual harassment that people have undergone over the years. On a par, as far as dehumanizing experiences, are the cattle calls, or open casting sessions. In these sessions, open calls go out for actors of a certain type, and the result is a room overflowing with blondes, or tall men, or obese people, or whatever the call was intended to turn up. Actors are shuttled in and out like cattle, and usually given no more than a cursory look or listen to by the individuals holding the casting call. This kind of experience can be very discouraging, but is all too often a necessary first step for the actor looking for his "break."

If one does get a chance to be interviewed for more than a few seconds, it is important to make the right impression. Those conducting the interview should be left with an indelible impression of what your personality is like. For the most part, your looks are your looks. Obviously you should show up appearing your best. But from there, the impression you convey is based in large measure on the personality you project. Most coaches will instruct their students to be themselves. This is generally good advice. However, if you are very quiet and introverted by nature, you might consider adopting a different persona for interview purposes.

Many actors will dress up for the interview, donning clothes to look like the character role for which they are reading or interviewing. There is nothing wrong with this approach, and it has often proved successful for acting hopefuls. It is never a sure thing, however, as Sean Young discovered when she dressed as the Cat Woman trying to land the part in *Batman Returns*, only to see the part given to Michelle Pfeiffer.

In most cases, actors trying out for motion pictures will not have the opportunity to read the entire screenplay. Even if cast in the film, if it is a minor role, they will probably be given only the pages containing their scene, known in the business as "sides." This is one of the points of departure from the theater, where the script is usually distributed to the entire cast. The logic is, of course, that the minor actor will not be present for the entire shooting, but only to do his scenes. His motivation and actions are fully contained in the pages in which he appears, and those are all that are given to him.

Many actors find that it is very helpful to their careers to study, or continue studying, after they arrive in Hollywood. There are a large number of acting schools and coaches listed in trade papers, in books on acting, and even in the telephone Yellow Pages. These programs are frequently organized around acting philosophies, from "The Method" to more representational techniques. They frequently indicate that instruction is based on the techniques of important drama coaches such as Herbert Berghof, Sandy Meisner, or Lee Strasberg. Most people would argue that it is less important whose teachings are followed than it is that the aspiring actor studies and continues perfecting his craft. Taking classes will also allow the actor to continue his networking efforts as well as find opportunities to showcase his skills in workshop presentations. While acting classes do cost money, they are probably essential. At a minimum, they allow you to do what you are in Los Angeles to do, and that is act. Among all the other pressures to find work and eke out a living until you get established, the acting class is often a true tonic for an actor—a place that he looks forward to going to as frequently as he can.

Motion pictures (and television) have always made room for

many, many kinds of actors, some formally trained, and others who were personalities or celebrities in other professions. Jessica Lange made the move from successful model to play the lead in *King Kong,* to become one of the most respected actresses of her generation. Fred Dryer rose to prominence as the zany defensive end of the Los Angeles Rams and was known for living in his van long before he was known as the star of television's "Hunter." In most cases, those who come to acting from other pursuits study diligently to achieve respectability in their new profession. As with anything else, the more time and effort they put into it, the better actors they become.

Directors know the range of their actors and stretch them as far as they can go. Years ago, I was on the set of an obscure film called *The Incident.* Among the cast was Ed McMahon, the former "Tonight Show" announcer. Director Larry Peerce needed a reaction of sheer terror from McMahon. McMahon labored mightily but was unable to summon up the right resources to convey the mood the director wanted. Peerce yelled "Cut!" and dragged Ed outside the subway car in which the scene was set. Throwing him against the car, Peerce screamed at poor Ed McMahon that he was ruining the entire movie. Ed paled and tried to stammer an apology. Peerce wouldn't hear any of it and dragged him back on the set and called for another take. With a menacing look at McMahon, Peerce yelled "Action!" Deeply shaken, McMahon proceeded to deliver exactly the performance the director desired. He did it not because he had suddenly become an actor but because he was utterly fearful, for that moment, of the director's wrath.

One of the most commonly heard complaints in Hollywood is that the roles available for women are not equal to the roles available for men. A look at the statistics takes this point still further. There are roughly twice as many male roles in films as there are female roles. If this weren't bad enough, other than prescribed SAG scale payments, men typically receive better compensation than do women. When a film like *Thelma & Louise* comes along, with two strong, well-defined female roles, there is tremendous competition among the Hollywood actresses for the parts. This again points out the paucity of challenging, unusual parts for women.

As far as compensation goes, it must be noted that this is first and foremost a business. People are compensated in terms of their market value. If a female star could command the worldwide box office of an Arnold Schwarzenegger or a Tom Cruise, then she would receive like compensation. The truth is that no American actress, not Meryl Streep, not Barbra Steisand, not Julia Roberts, and not Jane Fonda, commands that kind of following in the global marketplace. Foreign distributors know that a Meryl Streep film will have a certain cachet and will attract a certain following. But that is a far cry from doing the type of business generated by the major male stars. There are many explanations for this, from the parts that are written to the difficulty certain kinds of films, like musicals or sensitive character stories, have in attracting an audience in foreign markets. When this is coupled with the unmistakable sexism that is definitely a factor in Hollywood, it is clearly more difficult for an actress to achieve a high level of success than it is for an actor.

The problems of ethnic types are a further extension of the problems women face. At this writing, with the success in the summer of 1991 of *Boyz N the Hood*, it is a good time for black actors to find other than stereotypical roles in films. How long that will last is an open question. It has long been one of Hollywood's nastiest secrets that blacks and other ethnic minorities occupy almost no important executive seats or other positions of responsibility. Hopefully that is changing. With that change, and spurred by such facts as blacks' constituting 25 percent of the moviegoing audience, it is hoped that the coming years will see many more opportunities, at every level, for minorities and for women.

One of the difficult lessons to absorb as an actor is not to take rejection personally. This is very tough. As an actor, you go through your paces, letting it all hang out, and dropping all of your defenses for the sake of the role and the performance. If you are found unacceptable, it is a difficult pill to swallow. Those who make the casting decisions do so for any number of reasons. And they certainly make mistakes. In one film that I worked on, *The Lone Ranger*, the lead, a young man whose looks were very striking, was cast over the objections of many like myself who feared he didn't have the experience to play the part. His performance in production was disastrous, and ultimately every word of dialogue that he uttered was replaced by another actor. That problem did generate the most astounding suggestion I had heard in fifteen years in Hollywood. When I called the producer to express my alarm about the performance of the actor playing the Lone Ranger, he said he had a plan to "cover" for his acting inadequacies. Waiting anxiously, I was told that he intended to recast the film with bad actors so that the difference wouldn't be so pronounced. Yes, mistakes do happen, with surprising regularity, even on big, expensive films.

Should you be successful in landing a speaking part in a motion picture, you will, in all probability, choose to join the Screen Actors Guild. As the collective bargaining agent for actors, SAG assures its members everything from minimum payments to residuals and fair working conditions. Pension and welfare benefits, along with medical insurance, also go along with the benefits package. There are initiation fees and annual dues, but they are a small price to pay to belong to this guild.

In addition to gaining admission by virtue of having a line (or more) of dialogue to speak in a film, there are also ways to get in by using a previous union membership such as Actors Equity, AFTRA (American Federation of Television and Radio Artists), or AGVA (American Guild of Variety Artists). If you have obtained guild or union membership in another branch of the entertainment industry, you should make inquiries of SAG about the "parenting" procedures that allow you to join SAG.

SAG scale rates moved up to $448 per day and $1,558 for a week in 1991–1992. Industry practice sees these prices negotiated at scale plus 10 percent, the 10 percent going to the agent. Of course, this is the minimum payment made to an actor. At the other extreme, the star performer gets whatever price the market will bear. This can produce staggering compensation such as that commanded by Arnold Schwarzenegger or, in certain films, Sylvester Stallone, Tom Cruise, Michael Douglas, and a handful of others. At this writing, there are grumbles from the studios that the salaries of middle-range stars, those who do not have an automatic following with movie audiences, are overinflated. Whether any serious cutback in these prices will be made remains an open question. Viewed from the sidelines, the present salary levels make it a very advantageous time to consider the acting profession. Then again, when one notes what average pitchers and hitters are currently taking as salaries in major league baseball, maybe that line of work should also be given serious consideration.

Once having secured something of a foothold as an actor, which is to say, once you have begun to work regularly, you can begin climbing the ladder to artistic and financial success. Working, in and of itself, will be less important than selecting the right parts to further your career. By this time, you will be represented by an agent who should be of great assistance in finding parts, selecting the right ones, and taking care of the business end of things—from compensation to billing. With the chance to be more selective, you will be looking for better and better parts—those that give you an opportunity to grow as an actor, to stretch to play new kinds of roles, to change genres from drama to comedy and back, and to work with important directors and other actors. Hardest of all to judge is when a screenplay will become a hit movie. If you are able to make that determination, you probably should be running a studio and not running after acting parts. Most actors look for parts that allow them to demonstrate a wide range. They want their characters' arcs to progress from *A* to *Z*, and not from *A* to *B*. Too often, actors read screenplays looking only for their characters' lines. While this is certainly understandable, it is preferable to try to get a handle on the entire project.

Staying at the top, while a nice problem to have, can nonetheless be a real problem. Many are the actors who through combinations of wrong choices and bad luck lost their followings and the very audiences that elevated them to star status in the first place. Burt Reynolds went from being the nation's number-one box office star to acting in a series of blue-collar comedies. While not unsuccessful on their own terms, they stranded Reynolds high and dry, without his former audience support. It has taken many years for Reynolds to win back the hearts of Americans, and ironically he seems to be doing it through television and not through feature films.

Molly Ringwald seemed destined for superstardom after a series of compelling performances in early John Hughes films such as *Sixteen Candles*, *The Breakfast Club*, and *Pretty in Pink*. Her next choices, not only what she played but what roles she turned down, changed her fortunes dramatically and propelled her in the opposite direction. Plotting a career in this manner is less than an exact science. There is a large element of luck to it, but skillful guidance and good instincts are vitally important. One need look no further than the meteoric career of Julia Roberts to see what can happen when everything falls into place the way it is supposed to. Whether even that career has a degree of permanence is the more difficult question.

On balance, considering the unpleasant times and treatment that typify the beginning of most actors' careers, it is not surprising that they display fits of pique and temperament when they achieve star status. Significantly, some actors do not become monsters when they become stars. The "class act" will retain his professionalism at every level of the industry. Persistence, patience, and professionalism—those are probably the key words to hang on to if you are trying to make it as an actor. If those qualities are backed up by talent, you have a real chance to make it in the motion pictures.

PRODUCTION MANAGEMENT

If a movie crew were divided along military lines of command, the producer, director, cast, and screenwriter might be considered the officers. The technical personnel so necessary to get the job done would be the enlisted men. Standing in a unique position between these two groups would be the senior noncommissioned officer—the production manager. Part management and part labor, the unit production manager (UPM) occupies a special place on the roster of a movie crew.

The unit production manager is principally charged with monitoring the budget of the film and bringing the picture in on schedule. The department heads in all of the technical categories report to him and convey their successes and failures in meeting the budget allotments of their respective areas. The preparation of the initial budget figures represents the best guess of the production manager, based on his actual experience and on research of what things should cost. Only when these figures are tested by the department heads against the realities of the marketplace will there be an accurate understanding of the cost of the movie. Very little is cut-and-dried, however. There is much negotiating that takes place before the final numbers are set in stone. The production manager constantly examines and reexamines ways to mount the film at a better price. It is a task requiring skills in diplomacy and persuasion as well as years of experience.

The production manager does not function in a vacuum. While his task is to watch over the money, he must do so in the context of getting the director's vision of the picture on the screen. This is where the challenge of production management begins. Were the production manager working alone, the preparation of budgets and shooting schedules would not pose major problems. But the production manager does not shoot the picture. The director does. This fact introduces what is at once the great challenge of production management as well as the source of job satisfaction. Productions are virtually always constrained by having a limited amount of money with which to shoot. How that money is massaged, manipulated, and managed so as to provide the most available resources for the director is the art and science of production management.

If the budget is a finite amount of money, then an overage in any account must be offset against a saving from another account. The production manager wrestles with this problem on a continual basis. His task is complicated by the fact that department heads, up to and including the director, are always coming to him asking for more money. This money is not for personal compensation. In the movie business, unlike some others, rates of compensation are set at the outset of a film and are not usually altered. Requests for more funds have to do only with the cost of producing the film. In television, unlike features, the production manager typically says no to any such request. The issue of art or even quality is rarely a meaningful standard in that medium. The difficulty in motion pictures, however, is that requests for more funding are frequently accompanied by the argument that the picture will be qualitatively better if the additional money is spent. Implicit in the argument is the notion that a better film will do more business and produce greater profits. Sometimes, as with the request for more equipment, the argument is made that although there will be a budget increase now, there will be savings down the road. The picture will be finished faster; or the expensive star will be wrapped at an earlier date; or some other similar benefit will accrue to the production.

In feature films, there are rarely clear-cut and simple solutions to these kinds of problems. The production manager must endeavor to understand the aesthetic of the director and find a way with the available resources to implement it. In the motion picture *Barbarosa,* we worked with an Australian director, Fred Schepisi, shooting his first American film. Great pains were taken in the hiring of a production manager who could guide Schepisi through the problems he would face, while still allowing him to shoot in his unique directorial style. A production manager was chosen after considerable research and interviewing. He turned out to be the wrong man for the job. His competence and experience were everything that had been represented to us. He was unable to adapt, however, to Schepisi's singular ways of working. He kept insisting that Schepisi's plan was "unworkable," and "couldn't be done." Since it is the job of the production manager to effectuate the director's vision of the picture, the production manager had to be discharged during preproduction and replaced by someone with more flexible views. Subsequent experience proved that Schepisi's plan was indeed workable—if unusual.

The production manager is one of the first people hired when a picture has been given the green light for production. Sometimes his services will have been utilized before that time to prepare a budget and shooting schedule to facilitate the raising of money for an independent picture. Many production managers supplement their income by free-lancing the preparations of boards and budgets to assist independent producers and small production companies. For a studio picture, the production manager comes on board when the picture begins preproduction.

His first task is to break down the script, board it, and budget it. Taking the screenplay, he numbers each scene and organizes them into a logical sequence for filming. Films are not shot by beginning at page one of the script and continuing until the end. Instead, other financial considerations dictate the order in which films are shot. Day scenes are clustered together, as are night scenes. Scenes utilizing the same set are linked together, regardless of where they fall in the script. Scenes involving certain actors, especially highly-paid performers, are put in close proximity to one another. If you are paying an actor $1 million a week, common sense tells you to finish his scenes as quickly as possible and not let them drag out over the course of the shooting schedule. The shooting schedule is a complex puzzle involving many variables and shaped, at every turn, by financial considerations.

As the production manager works with these variables, he makes strips for each scene and assembles the strips onto a production board that is a blueprint for how the film is to be shot. He must review this board with the director to get his agreement on how long it will take to shoot each of the scenes. A mere line in a script such as, "They make love," may seem like two hours' work to the production manager, but more like two days' work to the director.

The production manager will be closely involved in the hiring of the crew for the film. Recommending those he has worked with before as well as those who enjoy good reputations, the production manager is instrumental in building the team to make the picture. He must give some attention to the ways the various department heads will blend with the director as well as with each other. The production of a film is a high-pressure experience, and if tempers fray, or if temperaments run wild, the production manager will be forced to deal with the problems as they occur.

The strategy for making the picture must be worked out at this time, and the production manager is again in the center of the decision-making process. Working with the producer and the director, fundamental questions must be answered. Will the picture be shot on location or at a studio? Will it be union or nonunion? Will it use practical sets or instead build sets on a stage? And will this be a big-budget film over $20 million, or one that is more reasonably priced? The constant shifting of these assumptions is what accounts for the five to twenty budgets that are made for most pictures produced today.

A large part of the production manager's work in preproduction involves the logistics required to move, house, and efficiently utilize the 125–150 people it physically takes to make a film. Deals must be struck with hotels, unions, independent contractors, caterers, and a wide variety of other specialists required in that particular film. Today's films tend to place great emphasis on incorporating visual effects. While agreements generally contain a fixed price for the delivery of the needed effects, the production manager is still required to be conversant with the territory and to make recommendations to the producer and the director.

As preproduction winds down, department heads will be focused on their own areas, and the production manager will be grappling with the overall problems regarding budget and schedule. As often occurs, when all the fat is squeezed out of a budget, the only way to reduce time and dollars further is by cutting the number of shooting days. The director must again be consulted to get his acquiescence in shifting the schedule around. In this fashion the production manager works closely with the producer in attempting to straddle the often competing interests of artistic needs and financial realities. There never seems to be enough money or enough days to make the film the way the creative group would like. Somehow, in a flurry of last-minute changes, the board and the budget are finalized and signed by the production manager, the producer, and the director.

For the production manager, production is the payoff to his many weeks of preparation. Production is the time in a movie's life when Murphy's Law is very much in evidence. That is, If something can go wrong, it will. For the well-prepared production manager, many of these problems will have been averted by careful planning during the preproduction period. It will still prove impossible for the production manager, no matter how well prepared, to avoid all unforeseen difficulties. The adroit production manager rolls with the punches and lands on his feet. He knows the amount of money that he has available to move through different accounts, and he juggles these accounts so as to accomplish the mutual goals of bringing the picture in on budget and paying for the film that the director wants to make. This is certainly not an easy task—especially amid the pressures of a film in production. Problems will arise from many quarters. There will be problems in meeting schedules and budgets, problems in personnel, and problems between the studio or other financing party and the unit making the film. In the eye of this storm, the production manager works to keep the good ship afloat. He must handle the inevitable complaints of the crew, who direct their problems to him as their immediate superior. He must also walk the tightrope between his reporting responsibilities to the producer and the director, and to the studio. Many production managers dread this arrangement as they are forced to serve two masters. Others take it in stride, understanding that the simplest and most trouble-free arrangement is to say the same thing to everyone. Honesty and straightforwardness will serve the production manager well as he summarizes his point of view for all of the interested parties. In many instances, he is not able to offer much more than an educated guess. The pace of the production, and its ability to meet its schedule, in the final analysis lie in the hands of the director. Studios are aware of this fact, and they look to the production manager only for educated guesswork. In an independent picture, the producer will be the only financial authority to whom the production manager will report. This may simplify the logistics, but the actual problems will remain the same.

When problems do occur in production, as is almost always the case, a resourceful and inventive production manager can be instrumental in helping the unit work its way out of difficulty. Most of his time is spent in the production office, on the telephone or on the computer. If the producer is present during production, they will frequently work together, dividing the tasks at hand. There is much ground to cover and the effective production manager wheels and deals his way through this terrain, ideally keeping the best interest of the film paramount in his mind.

Nowadays, he is aided in his work by the advantages that can be derived from the computer. In preproduction, software programs have facilitated making changes to budgets and schedules and saved many man-hours of time. In production, especially when filming on remote locations, the inability to know current financial information is a thing of the past. Before the computer, all costs were sent to the studio, and it was not uncommon for several weeks to pass before expenditures were made known to the unit on location. Today, budget figures can be compared to cost runs on a daily basis. The studio is aware at the same time as the production unit of all costs that have been incurred. Everyone is on the same page, and more efficient financial planning is the result.

Eventually, the problems of production will come to an end as the picture wraps. Then postproduction begins. The production manager supervises all of the postproduction activities, although often on a nonexclusive basis. Anywhere from sixteen weeks to six months can be spent finishing a film. Much depends on the speed with which the director is able to assemble the film and carry out the responsibilities of mixing the sound portion of the film. For the production manager, it is a time when costs traditionally run over budget levels. Often such overages occur with the blessing of the studio executives, who see the money spent as enhancing an already promising film. Since overages at this stage tend to be measured in the tens of thousands of dollars, rather than in the millions that may be involved in production overages, the production manager can do little more than exercise due diligence and let the chips fall where they may. His expertise may be very useful in structuring advantageous postproduction deals, but he is often unable to do much more than make recommendations to the director or the studio. By the time the film goes to the laboratory, the production manager's job is complete, and he is off to his next assignment.

For the individual interested in a career in production management, there are several paths to consider. In union pictures, the production manager is a member of the Directors Guild of America (the DGA). The trainee program of that guild (described in the chapter on directing) provides entrée to guild membership and to admission to the ranks of production managers. This route begins with acceptance as a trainee and progresses upward into the ranks of the second assistant directors, then first assistant directors, and finally to being a production manager. Many who wish to become production managers make the transition into production management after logging in their time as second assistant directors. They have learned how a movie set works during production, the logistics of moving a company from location to location, and the kinds of problems that can develop during production. By not progressing to the job of first assistant director, however, they have skirted the opportunity to work closely with the director and experience firsthand the kind of problems the director encounters that are of a creative nature. This experience can certainly be gotten at a later time, working on different productions, but it is useful to have under one's belt as early as possible.

This route through the DGA training program will require a considerable period of time. It is estimated that three to five years are required to move up to second assistant director and gain enough experience on the job to move laterally into production management. Many have made this progression and it is a historically sound way to acquire the requisite skills before moving into production management.

Other paths are also open to the attainment of the goal of becoming a production manager. Some have reached that position by coming up through the crew ranks as a location manager. The location manager works in the physical and logistic aspects of production. In addition to securing the necessary locations on which the director wants to shoot, he is also instrumental in handling the often difficult problems relating to housing, feeding, transportation, and obtaining film permits. He develops an expertise in problem solving that will stand him in good stead should he move into the ranks of production managers. In his role as location manager, he will have little to do with problems relating to talent or to the operation of the set. Experience in these areas, both of which are of great importance to the production manager, will have to come at a later time.

Other production managers have begun their careers working in the accounting end of the business. Every production carries accountants who deal with everything from payroll to petty cash. While their work is confined to the production office, they can still develop a sixth sense about where financial problems will lie. They learn, firsthand, how to red-flag budgetary difficulties, and often how to suggest creative resolutions to these problems. While the work of the accountant or auditor is but a part of the area of expertise for which a production manager must assume responsibility, it is an important part. The accountant must augment his skills with more practical production experience if he is to make the transition successfully.

Finally, a time-honored course pursued by many is to begin at the bottom as an unskilled production assistant and work your way up. This usually involves spending time in commercials and low budget, independent films where union personnel are not involved. In such environments, it is possible to perform certain jobs, often without title, or even significant compensation, and learn the requisite skills while on the job. This happens more frequently than one might think. On independent productions, a willing pair of hands, coupled with an industrious and ambitious outlook, are often more than ample calling cards. For the aggressive individual seeking to accumulate as much experience as fast as he can, this is a wonderful way to learn. Without the formal areas of staked-out turf that unions insist upon in the large-budget films, a newcomer willing to put in the hours and ask the necessary questions can learn a great deal about production quickly. The nonunion film is less concerned with issues like seniority and union jurisdictions and is instead focused on the task at hand—bringing the film in at the best price in the shortest number of days. The work is hard and the hours are long, but the rewards are many. Such projects offer the newcomer excellent opportunities not only to do his job but, by asking questions and by helping out, to learn the jobs of others. Much of film production work involves solving problems that tax the collective experience of all the senior crew members. It may be as silly a problem as how you keep clucking chickens quiet during sound takes (give them peanut butter) or as difficult as moving an entire company to a new and unforeseen location. For a senior person to be able to delegate some of his duties to an eager trainee or production assistant frees him up to concentrate on other problems. It is a system that benefits both the newcomer and the production.

As in any kind of crisis-management position, the production manager will benefit greatly from approaching each problem coolly and rationally. The more experience he can bring to bear, the better the probability he will solve the problem. The prospect of losing all, or even a significant portion, of a $200,000 shooting day is enough to daunt even the most experienced worker. For the beginner to work side by side with a capable, experienced production manager is a lesson that simply can not be derived from books.

Paul Kurta is an experienced production manager and producer who has perfected his craft in union and nonunion motion pictures. His experience encompasses commercials, industrial films, low-budget and high-budget features. He has also worked extensively in cable and network television production. In assessing what it takes to succeed in production management, Kurta, perhaps surprisingly, mentions first an ability to work well with other people. More than an ability to juggle numbers or any other related skill, Kurta emphasizes fundamental communication skills as the key ingredient to successful production management. In his mind, it is analogous to playing a team sport. Different roles fall to different people, and everyone must be prepared to give up some of himself for the sake of the whole entity. The analogy is an apt one. Anyone who has ever been on a movie set has seen that the cast and crew members all wear T-shirts, belt buckles, and caps that designate them as members of that movie company.

With the blending of the different individuals into a cohesive group comes a sense of morale that is reflected in production efficiency and a spirit of cooperation. This is evidenced in many ways by a crew. It can be shown by something as simple as waiving a meal penalty so that a key setup can be completed. Or it can be manifested by a sense of professionalism that causes crew members to work to the best of their abilities rather than sloughing off their efforts and collecting their salaries.

At the center of the administration of the crew is the production manager. He may be assisted and supported by the producer and the first assistant director, but on most film crews it is the production manager whose organizational and communication skills are constantly put to the test.

Continuing, Kurta believes that the effective production manager must also have or develop entrepreneurial skills. It will fall to the production manager to solve the many production difficulties that each film inevitably must face. While his experience will certainly stand him in good stead, he will also have to show unbridled initiative to balance all of the pressures that will be swirling around him. Again, the answers are not to be found in textbooks. Resourcefulness, imagination, persuasiveness, ingenuity—these are the kinds of skills that must be demonstrated if the film is to have a chance at realizing both its artistic vision and its financial assumptions. As part of his entrepreneurial skill, the production manager must be extremely flexible in his planning. Plans are one thing. Films have a nagging habit of refusing to follow carefully worked out plans and schedules. The unexpected event or occurrence often intervenes, throwing all plans up for grabs. Such surprises put a premium upon the production manager who has the flexibility and resourcefulness to work out of these difficulties.

The job of the production manager, then, is not for the faint of heart. It requires a steadying hand, good interpersonal skills, experience, and a sense that every film is a continuation of a learning process. How one progresses on that learning curve will be the surest indicator of how good a production manager one has become.

Suppose all of this comes to pass. With success and a wealth of experience as a production manager, what horizons lie beyond this position? Many production managers are quite content to spend their lives in performance of these duties. Each film will pose different problems, and it is rare that boredom will ever set in. Others seek above-the-line status and move into the producing ranks. In today's Hollywood, with its emphasis on deal makers and agents, there are numerous entrepreneurial producers who simply do not know their way around a movie set. They may be very skilled at assembling salable packages, or befriending the decision makers at the studios, but the vicissitudes of production hold little appeal for them. Pictures developed by such producers have come to rely on the services of a highly qualified cadre of production veterans who assume the title of executive producer, line producer, or co-producer, and who provide the leadership necessary to bring the picture home on budget. Individuals like this have typically hailed from the ranks of the production managers. They are the people to whom the studios look to preserve the integrity of the budget. They will have production managers working for them, but they now function in broader realms. As studio budgets have risen in excess of $28 million, such individuals have become something of an elite force. They move from picture to picture, without suffering the frustrations of development hell. They deal only with "go" pictures, collect large fees and meaningful percentages of net profits, and work as much as they want to work.

The experienced production manager will often move laterally to take another position calling on his expertise. All studios (networks and cable companies) have production people in their employ whose job it is to oversee the physical production of the shows in production. They safeguard the corporate funds and work closely with their counterparts who are crewing the films themselves. The difference in the two positions is that the corporate production man has a fifty-two-week job with the same employer and doesn't have to wonder where he will find his next job.

A related position available to experienced production managers is to work for a completion guaranty company. The completion guarantor is the entity which, for a negotiated fee, agrees to put up any funds needed to complete a production in excess of 110 percent of its budget. As the completion guarantor is motivated to see that its funds are called upon as rarely as possible, it retains seasoned production veterans to oversee the operations of each picture that it guarantees. As with studio employment, the major point of distinction for the production manager is that he works for one company in a full-time managerial role.

In some instances, line producers reveal their below-the-line roots when they become very uncomfortable wrestling with problems of temperamental stars or vagaries of studio politics. In other cases, they readily don the sometimes gaudy colors of the producer and slip easily into all of his functions. What they will always have, which most producers do not have, is an intimate knowledge of the ins and outs of production. This background, with the skills they bring to the table, allows them to function as respected and important members of the motion picture community. What they bring to the table is real, as opposed to the stuff that dreams are made of, and their contributions to an economically troubled business are well respected and well compensated.

The task of production management, like most meaningful motion picture pursuits, used to be a male club, governed by the old boy network. Increasingly today that bias is breaking down. There are splendid female production managers in the business today, and with more and more frequency they are finding that the barriers to their obtaining work are breaking down. America seems to have lagged somewhat behind other countries in this regard, but important changes are now taking place. As more and more pressure is felt on budgets, people who are skilled at their work are judged on that criterion alone, and not on any issue turning on gender. As more women succeed to positions in above-the-line categories such as directing and producing, they will probably be instrumental in aiding women who have the requisite skills and expertise as production managers to realize their potential in this industry.

In the final analysis, a production manager can be nothing more than a naysayer. He can veto any burst of creative energy as being outside the budget and thus not practical (as frequently occurs in television). Or he can see his task in terms of the implementation of the vision of the director and strive to find a way to deliver that vision within his the budgetary constraints (more often the choice of feature-film producers and directors). The work is challenging, relentlessly stimulating, and, if one seeks it, upwardly mobile. Production management will be a staple as long as there is production. It is a discipline that will provide great benefits to its practitioners and can greatly benefit the overall success of each and every film.

BELOW-THE-LINE ARTISTS

The term below-the-line is derived from the production management side of the business. On a film budget, there is presumed to be a line that separates the creative players—the producer, the director, the screenwriter, and the cast—from the rest of the technical people who will physically make the movie. To divide people along the lines of creative and technical is, of course, absurd. By and large, the creative people are technically very gifted; and, in many instances, the technical people are so creative as to be also truly gifted. Still, the term below-the-line is in common usage and there is a general agreement as to which artists the term refers to.

Historically, the production manager has the least control over the fees paid to the above-the-line personnel. For that reason, most preliminary budgets reflect only the below-the-line departments—the actual physical costs necessary to make the film. Yet even these numbers are subject to some degree of variance in today's film world. Except in low-budget situations where the prices the producer can pay are determined by the amount of money on hand, certain below-the-line department heads are considered so important to the creative success of the picture that their compensation is subject to reasonably large salary swings. This development is a product of modern times. Only today are certain categories, among the technicians, broken out and treated with particular care and handling. In part, this represents a belated inclination to view film as art instead of a product turned out by a studio factory. It is also a long overdue recognition of the creative role played by individuals like composers and editors in the preparation of the final version of the film.

BELOW-THE-LINE ARTISTS

There are at least four department heads who make particularly important contributions to the creative content and overall success of a motion picture. These individuals are the director of photography or the cinematographer, the production designer or art director, the editor, and the composer. Their salaries in the marketplace reflect the demand for their services, and their contributions to the final product are regarded accordingly. Indeed, it is currently very fashionable for film critics to single out their specific contributions in reviews, commenting on how much the final film owes to their services. As the individuals at the top of these professions are regarded as artists in their own right, it is worth examining the route they have followed and what might lie ahead for a prospective artist in each of these professions.

To come up through the ranks and become a cinematographer is, like succeeding anywhere in the picture industry, difficult but by no means impossible. It is certainly easier in most cases to earn a living as a cinematographer than as a film director. Still, the field is always crowded with aspirants. Many of these individuals have nurtured for years the dream of shooting movies. Maybe they began with a still camera. Perhaps they worked up to 8mm or even 16mm. As time went on and consumer-grade videotape became widely accessible, perhaps they further sophisticated their skills working in the tape medium. In any event, they are now in the marketplace and much can be learned by charting their experiences.

Someone who says he has wanted to shoot movies since he was four years old is Richard Nezvadovitz. Now in his twenties, he is currently finishing his college degree, majoring in motion pictures. He did, however, take two years off to dedicate himself to the film business, and more particularly the camera department. Helped out financially by his parents, he nonetheless carved a niche for himself in Florida and the Southeast and began to earn very respectable money.

To get his foot in the door, Nezvadovitz did what many had done before him: he "hung out" and tried to get whatever apprentice work he could. Money wasn't important. Acquiring knowledge, experience, and contacts was. In time, his enthusiasm, energy, and talent began to be recognized. What he was doing as an unpaid apprentice evolved into paid positions on the camera crew. He logged in his time as a second assistant cameraman, then moved up to first assistant. Film was film. Whether the project was a commercial, an industrial, a public service announcement, or a low-budget feature, Nezvadovitz tried to keep working and keep learning.

It was quickly apparent to him that the more he knew about dismantling and assembling 16mm and 35mm cameras, the more valuable a crew member he would be. He took maintenance courses offered by camera manufacturers and he spent time assisting in camera repair facilities. Again, he was in the fortunate position whereby the money he earned was less significant than the experience he gained. In time he acquired his own camera which, when he rented it out, became another source of income to him.

While his work as a camera assistant is certainly not as glamorous as the work of a cinematographer, the experience is invaluable. Cleaning cameras, loading and unloading film magazines, keeping records of exposed film, changing lenses, pulling focus for the camera operator—all of these jobs are part of the education of a cameraman.

Inevitably, as with other positions in the picture business, a lot depends on the personal contacts that are developed on the job. The apprentice or assistant cameraman beginning his career will find employment when his services are requested by a cinematographer. Once becoming an established member of a camera crew, the assistant can usually work whenever his department head, the cinematographer, works.

In the case of Nezvadovitz, he wrestled with a problem that has nagged at many before him. He had left school to work in the industry and developed a certain momentum and ability to earn money. Finishing college was, however, very important to his family. After much soul-searching, he opted to come back and finish his bachelor's program at the University of Miami. While he does have the opportunity to shoot student films and work on an occasional commercial, his career is essentially on hold. As he describes it, he will have to reestablish contacts and rebuild the momentum he had established almost as if he had never worked professionally at all.

Training for work in the camera department can be gotten from film schools (although not typically in 35mm). Many would say this is as good an overall background as one can get to prepare for a career in cinematography. Most cities also have a camera shop where much can be learned about the technology of different cameras. The aspiring cameraman should not ignore the written word as well. Numerous books, equipment manuals, such periodicals as *American Cinematographer*, or even *Premiere Magazine*, shed valuable insights into advancements in the field.*

In time, with talent, the right preparation, and the inevitable good breaks, the assistant can move up to director of photography or cinematographer. Putting an ability to work well with people to one side, the D.P. has to have a marvelously trained eye. He must be able to take dazzling pictures that will delight his audiences and please his director. For the most part, he must also build his level of experience until he can get those pictures extremely quickly. Those who have visited movie sets know that most of the time is spent waiting for each shot to be lighted and prepared. The faster the cinematographer is able to achieve the vision of the director, without sacrificing his ability to take pretty pictures, the better his reputation will be in the industry.

Nezvadovitz, at this early stage of his career, believes his aesthetic sense, his eye, is far more sophisticated than his speed. He feels that through several more years of on-the-job experience he will learn how to light faster and more economically and thus

*For an excellent overview of the subject, see Cheshire, David. *The Book of Movie Photography*. New York: Alfred A. Knopf, 1987.

increase his value to a production. Many well-known cinematographers never develop any speed in lighting a set. Suffice it to say that the time they spend drives the cost of a film up to the point where they become the bane of production managers and producers and anyone who worries about costs as well as the film's look.

The great cinematographers in the world today hail from many different countries. It is not at all unusual to see a Swedish cinematographer shooting a Woody Allen film, or French or British or Italian cameramen working on Hollywood pictures. Their skills are not defined by national borders, but rather by their aesthetic talents and their speed on the set.

Most, but not all, camera people begin their careers working nonunion jobs. Work is more plentiful and it is generally easier to break in on nonunion shows. For many years, gaining admission to the union was extremely difficult. Since all studios are union signatories and thus require union personnel on their films, moving upward in this profession posed very real problems. At the present time, however, the International Photographers Guild—that branch of the I.A.T.S.E. union representing cinematographers, operators, assistants, and video camera classifications—has thrown open its doors to anyone who has worked in a film or video camera classification for 100 days over the past three years. This is a major breakthrough for many aspiring camera people. In some cases early in one's career, as with Nezvadovitz, the choice may be made not to join the union. Working principally in Florida, Nezvadovitz is generally employed on nonunion shows. He feels that at this stage of his career a union card might impede his working on a regular basis.

Unfortunately, the way is not as open for women who wish to gain acceptance as cinematographers. There are only a few women who are active in the union camera departments, although of course the union denies any kind of gender discrimination. The old arguments that women aren't drawn to crafts requiring a high degree of scientific technology, and that the assistants' jobs require a strength factor with which most women have difficulty, are often heard when the charge of discrimination is leveled. Dismissing those arguments, it is clear that this is one branch of the film industry where the boys' club mentality is alive and well.

Not so in the craft of film editing. Throughout film history, there have always been women who have enjoyed the fruits of being considered masters of the editing profession. Today there are many women editors as well as assistants moving up. Still, those in the profession can point to many male editors who will not work with female assistants. Since an editor chooses his assistants, this can pose a real hurdle for women in the marketplace. Happily, it is not the standard.

The editor has come to be regarded as a vital cog in the creative process of making a film. Not simply a cutter who assembles footage presented to him, the editor works with the director balancing the nuances and subtleties of how long each shot should appear in the film, where the emphasis in the scene should be placed, and how the transitions from shot to shot should be made. So important is this process that it frequently determines whether the audience will find a joke funny, a moment terrifying, or the scene heart-rending. In this sense, the coverage of a scene represents the raw materials, but the cut footage is the finished product.

Because the editor is intimately involved with the director in making each sequence of the film "work" so that the audience responds as intended, the editor is truly at the heart of the creative process of a film. Perhaps for that reason, more editors have succeeded in making the shift to being successful directors than members of any other film craft. Such distinguished directors as Robert Wise, Hal Ashby, and Karel Reisz all began their careers cutting feature films. More than anything else, the editor is finally concerned with making the story work. By adding a sense of aesthetics, the editor can be a great collaborator with the director in the cutting room, trying new options and experimenting with new ways to assemble the footage. As with the rest of the creative process in filmmaking, the director has the last word in these discussions. If the editor has forged a close working relationship with the director, however, his influence on the process can be formidable.

The editing room must be a highly organized and carefully maintained office space. With hundreds of thousands of feet of exposed film to work with, outtakes and trims must be stored in a logical, careful manner where retrieval can be virtually instantaneous. The responsibility for the organization of the cutting room falls to the assistant editor(s). One such person is Beverly Pinnas. Graduating from film school in 1984, she has long nurtured the dream of being a film director. Following a year of production assistant work, Pinnas wanted to get closer to the creative process. As she had always been drawn to postproduction, she opted to move into editing. After a stint at a postproduction facility, she put in enough time to be able to enter the I.A.T.S.E. as an apprentice editor. In that capacity, she helped the assistant editors maintain the paperwork in the cutting room, as well as assisting wherever possible with syncing dailies. Rarely will an apprentice become deeply involved in a creative aspect of assembling the film, although periodically her opinions were sought or she was permitted to observe the solution of an editing problem.

After a year and a half as an apprentice, Pinnas was able to move up to being an assistant editor. As contrasted to earlier times when the editor was assisted by an assistant and an apprentice, the current trend is to hire both first and second assistant editors in the cutting room. The higher you progress in this hierarchy, the more creative input you are permitted to give. Much will be determined by your relationship with the editor. It is the editor who is hired by the director. The editor hires his own assistants. If you develop solid working relationships with one or more editors, then the assistant jobs will continue to be there and some measure of job security will be achieved. Depending on the size of the picture, it is possible to exceed assistant scale of $870 per week. For Pinnas, who is on good working terms with a number of editors, a yearly gross of around $52,000 is very much in the ballpark.

Some editors will permit their assistants to cut segments of a film. This experience is invaluable training. Pinnas doesn't expect, however, to derive her basic editing experience while working as an assistant on a union film. Those jobs she takes to earn money, gain some experience, and broaden her network of contacts. The real experience as an editor comes from low-budget films, student films, and any other footage for which she can serve as the actual editor. Money, in these instances, is not the prime motivator. Gaining experience in hands-on cutting is. Such experiences are vital both to developing a more sensitive eye and to building the speed with which you can cut a film. More than anything else, Pinnas sees the ability to edit quickly, especially in the high-pressure atmosphere of working with a director and responding to the demands of a studio, as a goal for which she must keep striving.

While there is some lateral movement between editing for television and editing for motion pictures, usually reputations are made in one medium or the other. An assistant editor at the level of Pinnas has often heard her peers express a fear of "being trapped in television." As with other technological or equipment-driven areas of the business, in editing it is clearly an asset to acquire some familiarity with as many tools of the trade as possible. For the editing community, this often means working with both film and videotape. While many first-rank editors will cut only footage with sprocket holes—film—many low-budget features do all their post work in videotape. Technology is moving very quickly in the field of digital editing of tape, and a familiarity with both videotape and film editing machines and techniques will be considered a major plus for someone starting out.

Pinnas emphasizes a point made often by those starting out today: it is extremely important to have some resources saved so as to be able to take positions for the experience and contacts they will develop, and not always be forced to make decisions because of one's economic circumstances. Many have climbed the ladder of success without the benefits of having some measure of support in the early years; Pinnas, however, simply states that it is preferable to have some help in the first few years, if at all possible.

With some years of experience behind her, Pinnas now feels she has reached a modest crossroads in her career. Ahead is the transition to becoming an editor. Or perhaps she might rekindle her dream of becoming a director. At this writing, she expects to enter the AFI Directors' Program and earn an M.F.A. She feels her work in the cutting room has furthered her understanding of film and how it works, as well as introducing her to a large number of film community members. While the decision is not irreversible, she does believe that this is the time to focus her energies on becoming a director.

Another singular contribution to the success of a film is the work done by the art director or production designer. The latter title has grown in recent times to connote more authority or experience than that of art director. On large films, it is not uncommon to have a production designer with several art directors working for him. Many films get along very well with a department head called an art director. Production designer or art director, their basic tasks are the same. They are responsible for assisting the director in finding the "look" of the film. The conceptualization of the film's look encompasses everything seen on the screen. From sets to colors, costumes to props, the director must focus the attention of the production designer in a given direction. Often, this will be a matter of the production designer's making a series of suggestions from which the director chooses. At other times, the director will have a very clear idea what he wants, and the production designer must implement that vision.

The production designer's tasks are circumscribed by the constraints of the budget. It is not difficult to construct lavish period surroundings with a large budget. It is another question altogether when the budget for the art department is capped at a figure that requires some creative resourcefulness to "sell" the look to an audience. The best of the art directors are those who combine original bursts of creative expression with a solid sense of cost control.

The production designer will work closely with the set decorator, the scenic designer, and the costume designer. It is a single vision that is being fulfilled—that of the director. Inevitably, there is a managerial aspect to being a production designer as an entire department must function under his leadership.

The impact, financially, of the art department is not lost on the producer and the unit production manager. This department is traditionally a dangerous one from the standpoint of meeting budgetary expectations. Not only does it have a tendency to go over budget, but it has the potential to go *way* over budget. Anyone who has ever tried to bring a house construction project in on budget knows some of the problems that can beset an art department in a film. It requires a deft touch to achieve the required balance between imagination and cost-consciousness.

One individual who has achieved this balance on a number of films is Philip Harrison. An Englishman, he attended art school in London, graduating in 1964. After learning about his field in the design department of an independent television company in England, he got his chance to be art director for the well-regarded English film *Morgan!* Now based in Los Angeles, his work has included such films as *Outland, Blue Thunder, Mississippi Burning*, and *Bird on a Wire*. Harrison's work spans many genres and periods. He prides himself on being an "all-arounder," someone who delights in the challenges of different projects. Some production designers view their work in this fashion, while others lean more to specialization in a single look or genre.

Many times directors ask Harrison to work with them again. He acknowledges that "it is nice to be asked back." On the other hand, he welcomes the challenge of working with a different personality. In this sense, Harrison is typical of many artists in the business. Their relationships with other people such as directors are of great importance to them personally and professionally. Yet it is finally their own level of professionalism on which they rely.

The top echelon of production designers often have agents who secure work for them and negotiate their deals, as do the top cinematographers and editors. Sometimes they are represented by larger agencies, but more often by smaller, boutique agencies specializing in one or two technical branches. A top production designer can make around $200,000 for a picture, which explains why agents are interested in representing them.

As in the theater, which is a frequent training ground for film production designers, there seems to be very little gender discrimination in the art department. Talent rises to the top and is paid equitably along the way. Newcomers can find several avenues available to work in this area of the business. While job categories are quite rigid with the big union pictures, there are many nonunion films and other similar opportunities for the aspiring art director to get valuable experience. Even in colleges and universities, course work and film and theatrical presentations offer wonderful opportunities for the beginner.

At the entry level on a feature film, the beginner can expect to do what has to be done—from serving as a runner to doing drawings of smaller details. When Harrison hires, he looks to see the applicant's work. Specifically, he is interested in architectural drawings, or any graphic representations. Almost as important for him is what the applicant has to say about his work. He hopes to discover a good general background accompanied by a solid grounding in common sense. As mentioned, this is a pressure-filled area of a picture and Harrison is not looking for an explosive personality, even with dashes of brilliance. This is especially true at the entry-level positions, where a more pedantic quality is often necessary to bring a set to completion, at or under budget.

While sketches and models will certainly precede actual construction, Harrison emphasizes that it is important to be able to communicate one's ideas successfully in words. The better the production designer and the director can communicate while working closely together, the more cohesive and efficient the art department will be. On a picture of any size and scale, this has a major impact on the budget as well as the look of the film.

Any discussion of major contributors to the success of a film must include the composer. Again, as with the other important artists, his skills are directed toward realizing the director's vision of the film. As with the other key positions, budgetary constraints may be prominent in any discussion of music for a film. Not only do the top composers attract a great deal of money in today's market, the actual sound that is desired may vary greatly in price. It is one thing to discuss a simple electronic score for a film. It is quite another to speak of a full orchestral sound. The range in prices (although not the amounts) varies, as in hiring actors. It is possible to deliver the master on a complete score for $25,000, or even less. It is also possible to see numbers approximating $1 million under the budget item called Music.

The importance of music to a film is unquestioned today. The score enhances the emotional impact of the picture, whether it is designed to help provoke laughter, terror, or tears—or all of these emotions. It is composed (and often conducted) by a skilled, trained musician who is able to adapt his talents to the unique requirements of scoring a motion picture. To accomplish this end, the composer "spots" the cues with the director, developing the rough timings of where the director thinks music belongs. What style of music, from jazz to classical, is discussed with the director, and, of course, it is the director's call what kind of music will finally be included in the film.

Enormous discipline is demanded of the composer, since he must adapt his music to the precise timing of the scenes as they appear in the final version of the film. If the music is intrusive, it is defeating its very purpose. The music is generally intended, along with the sound effects, to enhance and support the dialogue and action of the story. Hence, an overwhelming score fails in its objective. To accomplish what a fine film composer should do requires a broad musical background. Many musicians are classically trained before specializing in one kind of music or another. Still others are formally trained in film composition in colleges, universities, and technical schools throughout the country.

Unfortunately, when they arrive in Los Angeles they will not be greeted with a warm reception. Film scoring is another field that is exceedingly tough to crack. This is particularly the case, perhaps surprisingly, for women. Charles Ryan, a Los Angeles agent who represents composers exclusively, estimates that there are no more than 200 composers who earn a living doing all the composition for motion pictures and television. Of that number, only two or three are women, and they are not preeminent in the field. Other than the fact that musical composition has historically been male-dominated, it is difficult to understand the gross disparity between men and women working in this area. Ryan states that even the tapes and inquiries about representation that he receives are predominantly from men.

What should the aspiring composer do to break into this area? As with many of the creative disciplines, there are no easy answers. Five or six agencies are primarily responsible for the representation of almost all of the composers who work regularly in the mediums of film and television. As with other disciplines, television is a field where one can earn a handsome living, but it is very difficult to move to motion pictures after establishing oneself as a television composer. According to Ryan, most composers prefer motion pictures, where the larger budgets and greater creative license offer more challenges and opportunities.

Since most agents are not looking to increase their client list, except with established composers, the odds are somewhat stacked against the new composer. Ryan counsels aspiring composers to keep plying their craft wherever they can. Score documentaries, industrials, student films—whatever is available. The money, he suggests, should not be the most important factor. The experience gained, the chance to broaden the base of industry contacts, and the opportunity to build a better sample tape are the goals that should be kept in mind. Frequently the young composers will meet a director on the way up and their relationship will blossom into collaborations on bigger and bigger pictures.

Ryan makes it a point to listen to the tapes that are submitted to him, but he confesses there is rarely anything he can do to help the submitter besides giving him advice. As Ryan points out, the days when knowledgeable musicians, like Lionel Newman at Twentieth Century Fox, supervised the music for studio films are long past. Today, these positions are held by former executives from the record companies whose emphasis is more on marketing than on music. This leads to a less adventurous attitude in the hiring of composers. Without the solid musical background necessary to "discover" new talent, these executives tend to go with established composers and simply place their bets on existing track records.

Ryan clings to the belief that this is a field where talent will out. Because success comes also from effectively collaborating with a director, the formula for rising to the top seems to include both personality and talent. In some instances, according to Ryan, certain composers are limited by their own abilities. It is undeniably helpful to have a sense of musical composition in films through the years. Similarly, it is helpful for the composer to have a grasp on the ingredients that account for the success of different film genres. It is said of good scriptwriting that the story seems inevitable and yet surprising. The same can be said of good film scores. The unexpected use of classical themes, as in Kubrick's *2001: A Space Odyssey*, or the many and varied strains of a Bernard Herrmann score, can be cited to illustrate the range and quality of compositions for the screen.

The composer is assisted in his labors by copyists, arrangers, and music editors. It is certainly possible for the beginning composer to consider working his way into the business by pursuing one of these avenues. Unlike in other crafts where apprenticeships with established artists are often the preferred route to follow, however, this direction is not generally open to composers. There are, of course, exceptions. Sometimes composers will utilize the service of young composers to assist them with their commitments. Too frequently, no credit is given the young composer for his efforts, and he has to take his minimal salary and chalk up the exercise to experience. This is not altogether bad, but it is undoubtedly a difficult spot in which to spend too much time.

Ryan reports that he is frequently the recipient of videocassettes that include scored footage from some kind of film or tape. He says that he and his colleagues, whether agents or filmmakers, will rarely take the time to view the whole cassette. He therefore urges that the tape be edited to no more than twenty-five minutes, that the cues depicted represent as great a variety of different musical themes as possible, and that the best cues be put at the head of the tape. To locate them in any other portion of the tape is to run the grave risk that they will never be listened to by the person to whom they were sent.

Finally, Ryan's advice to the composer starting out is to be as diversified as possible. This includes a more than passing familiarity with electronic music. Especially for lower-budget films, the music budget may not be large enough to accommodate anything more than an electronic score. The more expertise the beginning composer has in this area, the better.

These four categories of cinematographers, editors, production designers, and composers are all major contributors to motion pictures. While their work may not be fully appreciated by the average member of the audience, it is clear that they are pivotal in the creative process and instrumental in the audience's enjoyment of the film. All except the composer are members of a guild affiliated with the I.A.T.S.E. union. Composers usually belong to one of two major associations, A.S.C.A.P. and B.M.I., which provide a royalty structure for them. In general they are very well paid for their labors.

Representation by agents has helped push their wages up. Other forms of recognition such as Academy Awards or honorary societies such as the A.S.C. (American Society of Cinematographers) for cinematographers or the A.C.E. (American Cinema Editors) for editors have further enhanced their reputations as artists and not merely technicians. These professions have earned the respect of the picture community and the compensation that frequently accompanies such respect. Their creative contributions to the films they work on is well accepted. If you are considering one of these avenues to pursue, a rich and rewarding career could well stretch out in front of you.

THE TECHNICIANS

In addition to the well-publicized talents of the composer, the cinematographer, the editor, and the production designer, there are a host of technicians and craftsmen whose talents and skills are employed in the production of a film. Often unsung heroes, they are called by such titles as grips or gaffers or focus pullers or script supervisors. Their functions often seem like a mystery to those outside the industry. Yet their roles and talents are well known and widely appreciated, throughout the industry, for their contributions to film production are tremendous.

On a studio film, virtually all of the technicians will be members of different branches of the International Alliance of Theatrical Stage Employees (I.A.T.S.E.). Popularly abbreviated to I.A., this union has historically operated under the philosophy that by keeping its membership small, it could guarantee its members employment. In most branches, especially in New York, Los Angeles, and Chicago, it was exceedingly difficult to obtain membership in the union. Without the union card, skills notwithstanding, it was virtually impossible for a technician to find employment on a union film. Since all of the major studios were—and still are—signatories to exclusive agreements with the I.A., nonmembers were virtually frozen out of the marketplace.

For the newcomer, this often had disastrous consequences. The union films emanating from the studios usually carried the biggest price tags and brought the greatest financial and career-enhancing rewards. Without a card, the technician had no chance of getting work on a union show. Hence, newcomers had to look to nonunion films. Union shows did, however, suffer from the strictest kind of jurisdictional organization. A member of the electrical union (or even the producer trying to be helpful) could not move a piece of equipment from one side of the stage to another. This work was that of the grip, and the result of an action of this kind would probably be a union grievance, the imposition of a fine, or worse. Sets function very differently in a nonunion context. Without strict categories of labor defining who could do what, the task at hand became preeminent. Someone willing to pitch in and help with some chore on the set would find his efforts appreciated rather than punished.

For the newcomer, moreover, the nonunion environment provided a laboratory to acquire much needed experience. The assertive newcomer could learn more and do more on a nonunion set than would ever be possible on a union set. He could pitch in wherever his help was needed, crossing over jurisdictional lines with an ease and facility totally absent in a union environment. In terms of logging in experience quickly, nothing could rival the nonunion environment.

Today the thinking of many branches of the I.A. union has undergone a radical shift. Admission to the union has become far simpler to achieve, and (with some important exceptions in certain locals in Los Angeles, Chicago, and New York) the union has opened itself to new blood. Not every technician sees it in his best interest to join, however. Some individuals, especially those working in right-to-work states (such as Florida), believe that there is more nonunion work to be found than there is union work. The right-to-work statutes provide that nonunion personnel can not be excluded from a union set. Traditionally the existence of experienced nonunion crews in an area acts as a magnet for low-budget productions, whether from this country or from abroad. Should nonunion personnel wish to move up to the larger Hollywood studio features, however, they will still find that union membership is imperative—but the present union is much more open, to everyone's benefit.

For the person starting out, a job is a job is a job. Long-range thinking is less important than the short-term necessities of providing minimal sustenance. If the technical area is examined from this perspective, certain conclusions can be drawn. The traditional starting place for many is the job of production assistant, also called a gopher (or go-fer). Routinely given to someone off the street or someone with a college degree, or even a graduate degree, this position is at once difficult to get and frequently frustrating when one does get it. The P.A. is the low man on the totem pole, doing what he is told to do, from photocopying files to fetching coffee to running errands for almost anyone who asks him. The job is notoriously low paying (if indeed it pays anything), with very long hours and little promise in the way of creative opportunity. But it does get one's foot in the door. It can get one exposed to a wide variety of different people—from production managers to cinematographers—any of whom may take a liking to an enthusiastic and aggressive work style. The possibilities for advancement, especially on nonunion films, are dramatic.

Since the P.A. job is itself a nonunion and nonskilled position, there is a great crush of applicants for these positions, especially on the big, glamorous Hollywood films. More often than not, the job is given out as a favor to the child of a prominent figure—a producer or studio executive—or to someone who had the good fortune to be in the right place at the right time. While often difficult to land, these positions are still worth trying to get. One tip that may help those in areas outside of Los Angeles and New York: stay in close contact with your local film commission. Every state, and many counties and cities, have film commissions charged with attracting film productions to their geographic area. They will be aware of a unit's coming to shoot weeks and even months before the crews arrive. The trick is to get the name of the production manager who will be hiring P.A.'s long before he leaves Los Angeles for your area. Write, call, fax, do whatever you can do to get your name in front of him *before* he arrives. If he is impressed with your aggressiveness and persistence, you stand a good chance of moving to the front of the line and being hired.

The other technical areas offer a wide range of work experiences covering diverse talents and skills. For those dealing with equipment, grips, electricians, and others, some aptitude for and experience in mechanical and electrical work is useful if not indispensable. Machine shop experience, carpentry experience—these skills and related technical backgrounds stand one in good stead for motion picture employment. It is important to note that there is no shortage of manpower in any of these areas, and so the applicant who knows working members of the union or other working nonunion personnel in these fields stands a better chance of getting hired. As is consistent with the entire industry, in all of its job categories it is often who you know as much as what you know.

Many young people are drawn to the field of makeup after seeing the minor miracles brought about on the screen by Hollywood's makeup wizards. These newcomers frequently experience disappointment when they discover that the overwhelming number of makeup jobs in motion pictures offer nothing more challenging than readying an actor or actress to go in front of the camera in modern-day dress looking presentable. There are simply not many special makeup jobs available, and those that are around tend to go to the most experienced artists. Those who have worked on a set know that the makeup and hair people are often the first to be called for work in the morning because they have to ready the actors for the first shot. If special makeup is called for, they may also be the last to leave if the actors need help getting their makeup off.

If the newcomer has long nurtured the dream of building appliances and working in plastics used to manufacture the makeup creations seen in science fiction or horror films, it must be understood that patience and experience will both be required. There are courses given in these special skills, as well as books that provide assistance and instruction for the newcomer.* As with many other crafts in the picture business, it is a mistake to consider only major Hollywood films as workplaces. Small independent films, from low-budget features to student films, often provide wonderful opportunities for the newcomer to work on his craft. Film or tape of the results of these labors is often the best résumé one can have to find future employment in this field.

Equally valid as a way to get one's foot in the industry door is the possibility of apprenticing for someone with extensive credits. Sometimes these positions will pay a salary, sometimes not. Much, therefore, will depend on the individual's financial needs. If you are fortunate enough to secure an apprenticeship in makeup, or some other discipline, the chance will be there not only to learn from a master, but also to expand a list of contacts that will one day help you secure employment on your own. Both the experience gained and the personal contacts are of almost equal importance. The movie industry remains a business where it is frequently who you know that paves the way for your progression through the ranks. Many before you have started from ground zero, knowing no one, possessed only of a passion to learn and advance as quickly as possible. By application of your talents, demonstration of initiative, and unflagging enthusiasm in the workplace, your upward movement is assured. There is always a luck factor in so far as timing or other considerations not controllable by you are concerned. Luck tends to balance out over the long haul, however, and more often than not, it is the capable, skilled workman who in effect makes his own luck.

An apprenticeship is probably the preferred route to learn many of the trades that attract young people to the business. The special effects department draws many newcomers, excited about the prospect of blowing up buildings or bridges, or working with

*An excellent overview is provided in Kehoe, Vincent. *The Technique of Film and Television Make-Up*. New York: Hastings House, Inc. 1969.

gallons of imitation blood. Much training is required, even for low-budget films, in the area of special effects. Education is a must, and there are often special licenses one must have obtained just to be allowed to perform the stunts demanded by the director. Mechanical skills and such practical knowledge as plumbing are part of the requirements for this branch of the movie business. While formal training programs are rarely available for interested beginners, informal apprenticeships are definitely a possibility. They can be secured only by patiently tracking down the active practitioners of this art and pleading your case as well as you can. If you are successful in getting someone to take you on as an apprentice, you are well on your way to securing a niche in the business.

Throughout the credits of a film, the viewer can see various departments, with department heads and staff, who have contributed to the final look and sound of the film. Skills ranging from sound to set decoration, from script supervisor to scenic designer, are to be found on industry rosters. Unless you have always been focused on a dream to occupy one position or another, one of the great advantages to gaining some entry-level job such as production assistant is that it affords the opportunity to observe what many different people do. While the job of the script supervisor, marking up a shooting script to keep a log of each take, from dialogue to dress, may seem almost clerical in nature, it is only when you see that they sit by the camera, adjacent to the director and the actors, that the job becomes somewhat more glamorous. This is not to demean the work of the script supervisor whose efforts are indispensable to the editor in postproduction as well as to the director during shooting, but only to indicate that much of the reward of any position comes from aspects of the working conditions that might not be readily apparent to the beginner.

Some positions seem to call into play talents or skills that you already possess. A background, educationally, on stage, or professionally in styling or design, may lead naturally to a position in motion picture wardrobe or costume design. As with many other areas, learned abilities in cost control, research, and imaginative styling will finally determine who the outstanding practitioners of this craft will become. The more background and experience you can bring to it, the better off you will be.

Some fields such as the camera department or the sound department demand a high degree of mechanical or electronic knowledge. Sound, of course, enters the process both in the recording of dialogue and other sounds during production, and also in the studio recording and sound mixing portions of postproduction. The more knowledgeable and talented the sound people and the engineers are, the better the sound portion of the film will be. While it is possible to effect major rescues of production tracks in the mix theater, it is always better to have good sound from the outset.

A worthwhile reference book in the area of sound, albeit with a particular emphasis on music, is Altan, Stanley. *Audio In Media*, Wadsworth Publishing Company; Belmont, California, 1990.

It should be emphasized with sound, as with all of the technical areas, that there are clearly defined levels of excellence and corresponding assessments within the industry as to who the great technicians are and who the journeymen are. To rise to the top of the profession in special effects, makeup, sound, camera, or almost any of the technical pursuits, is to have earned the respect of other professionals who know the difference. Usually, that measure of respect is accompanied by a commensurate rate of compensation.

Many of the skills that were needed in the former eras in Hollywood have tended to be less in demand as fashions in film have changed. While scenic designers and set decorators are still employed in films, the dearth of period films today has somewhat limited their imaginations and the skills they can employ. Even at the big studios, whole departments such as plasterers and sculptors have been let go as their services do not find outlets in many of today's films. In the world of scenic design, much can be learned in either the educational arena or the legitimate stage.

One technical area that deals closely with the producer and director, at least during the preproduction period of a film, is casting. The casting director supplies suggestions of new and established talent based on their abilities, price, and availability. Casting directors must constantly update their files as new people burst upon the scene, or more established people demonstrate a range of talent that was previously not known. The good casting director will have a distinct point of view regarding certain actors for certain roles and will fight to get his point across. He will be, above all else, a shrewd judge of talent with a particular eye for that mysterious ingredient called star quality. The well-cast film may not be noticeable because everyone seems correct and somehow fresh in his role. It is an aspect of good casting to avoid the cliché and to find new faces and talents. These skills in casting can be developed working for existing casting directors, or in related fields like the talent agency business. The newcomer is more likely to be asked to cover a small neighborhood theater presentation to check out the actors than he is to negotiate a major acting deal on behalf of a film. Yet, at the entry level, there will be an exposure to talent and to the filmmaking process. For many, it is the beginning of an exciting and rewarding career.

Perhaps not properly suited for inclusion in a chapter called Technicians are the stunt people—almost a category unto themselves. In this film era characterized by elaborate action-adventure sequences with major feats of apparent derring-do, stunt people are enjoying much prosperity. They work independently of the unions, preferring instead to affiliate in their own associations.

In a film that requires stunts, a stunts coordinator, usually someone with an extensive background in the field, will be hired to contract the rest of the stunt people. Not infrequently, a star will designate his own stunt double, someone who has done the stunts for him on many of his previous films.

Stunt people will have general athletic skills as well as individual specialties. These may range from driving to sword fighting, from boxing to horseback riding. Whatever the required action, there will be a ready pool of men and women who can stand in for the actors and carry out the stunts as the director requests. Because of the element of risk inherent in the job, the pay tends to be quite good. Stunt people receive a weekly (or daily) rate of compensation which is augmented by "stunt adjustments" for particular activities undertaken on the set. Ironically, the picture business downplays the risk factor by terming actions such as falls or crashes "gags."

Entry into this offbeat end of the picture business, for men or women, is available for those possessing the requisite athletic skills and fitness. Most gyms in the Los Angeles area have instructors who are familiar with active stunt coordinators. More help can be obtained from an association such as Stunts Unlimited [(213) 874-0050], which can put the beginner together with experienced movie veterans.

Stunt people are a special breed in the movie business, close-knit and highly professional. For a young person with excellent physical qualifications, this is a challenging and interesting avenue to explore.

There was a time, some years back, when the technical and crafts people had few complaints about the picture business. More frequently, in fact, the picture business complained that the unions were making life miserable for them by setting rates that were excessive and demands that were unfair. Today, except for the "stars" who command top dollar as cinematographers or editors or a handful of other positions, the average technical person is having second thoughts about continuing in the business. Brian Unger is an International Representative for the I.A.T.S.E. union. He has been a member of the union for nine years and worked directly for it for three. His point of view is uniquely appropriate regarding the shape of the marketplace today, since he is a 1981 graduate of New York University's motion picture program. Half-jokingly, he is wont to say to newcomers or college students inquiring about the technical side of the movie business today, "Find another line of work."

What has changed to take the edge off a career on the technical side of the street? What prompts Unger to offer this downbeat forecast, even with his tongue partially in his cheek? It is what he eloquently calls a "paradigm shift." As he sees it, unions have lost clout and bargaining power in the last ten years. Nowhere is this felt more acutely, he believes, than in the squeeze effected on the lower echelons of the union force by the studio policy of making local hires. In practical terms, this means that a studio film shooting, for example, in North Carolina, will hire personnel that show up on location. With certain exceptions, they are unwilling to pay transportation, housing, and per diems, as they used to do when they imported crews from Los Angeles or New York. While this clearly reduces some aspects of the film's budget, it puts a lot of pressure on the people at the bottom of the ladder to net enough take-home pay to make the disruption of family life worthwhile. The irony of the situation is that the overall cost of films keeps increasing as above-the-line salaries soar out of sight. The squeeze is made where the film companies believe they can safely make it—at the bottom of the economic ladder.

In addition, there is an inevitable process at work to simplify and lighten the equipment used to make a movie. In the parlance of today, it is more "user friendly." One of the less apparent consequences of this "progress" is that fewer technicians may be needed to accomplish the same job. This puts filming into the same category as many other industries in which members of the labor force are being squeezed out by refinements in technology that have rendered them redundant. For example, the large lights that used to be commonplace on a movie set can now be replaced by a small compact HMI light. With that transition, one person can do the job that used to require three.

Again, it must be emphasized that at the top of the technical world the most important personnel are doing fine. Their skills are not defeated by technological advancements and their services are in more demand than ever. Accordingly, their salaries are at all-time highs. It is the troops in the trenches who are suffering at this point.

Parallel with these changes is a dramatic shift in the philosophy of most of the technical unions from a craft union mentality to an industrial union way of thinking. This is manifested in the new, greatly relaxed entrance requirements. Although there are still some holdout unions maintaining their craft thinking, especially in Los Angeles and New York, the bulk of the unions within the I.A. have adopted the industrial model. This leads them to admit virtually everyone in the work force, instead of attempting to keep the union small and exclusive. This is probably working for the good of the industry and the good of the unions. Nonunion films and right-to-work states that allow union and nonunion personnel to work side by side conspire to defeat the craft mentality that used to be the hallmark of the I.A. system—and bode well for the newcomer, especially outside L.A. and New York.

Against this changing landscape, it is interesting to note that, at least to Unger's thinking real progress is being made to end some forms of discrimination that were endemic to the picture business. He feels that the last ten years have witnessed the addition of many more women to the motion picture labor force. He is quick to add that conditions are not ideal, but that genuine progress has been made in such formerly male bastions as grip and electric. When discussing past problems, Unger does add that it is unrealistic not to take into account the fact that some of these technician jobs require lots of hard physical work. As Unger succinctly puts it, "Being a grip is no job to have three-inch fingernails." In other words, the work involved is of a sort to which some people are not predisposed.

From Unger's perspective, the film industry is aligned with much of the rest of the nation's businesses. Progress against discrimination on the job is being made, but often not at the pace he would like. He would welcome more change in this realm, as he would in the country as a whole. Women and blacks have tended to see the fastest growth in the opportunities available to them in recent years, while Hispanics have not enjoyed the same breakthroughs. In part, according to Unger, this may be attributed to the gains women and blacks have made in the recent past in such above-the-line positions as director. Given the opportunity to hire, many women and blacks have been inclined to give other women or minorities a break.

An equally insidious, if less discussed form of discrimination is also present in the picture business, according to Unger: age discrimination. He feels that the employers would rather forgo a wealth of experience and hire a younger person in the belief that he will work harder for his hourly pay. Since the feature film business probably employs no more than 20,000 workers overall, lopping off members of the work force as they reach forty can have disastrous effects for the low-level technical people. This problem is of great concern to Unger and his I.A. colleagues. At this writing, they feel they have made few inroads into remedying this situation.

If Unger sees a ray of hope, it lies in the growth potential of some of the newer production entities. Specifically, he cites cable television, MTV, and low-budget filmmaking as picking up some of the slack for his workers. Unger is confident that people who do the proverbial honest day's work for a day's pay can look to these newer forms of programming both to reward the experience that older workers offer and to be more than satisfied with the work they perform.

As far as technicians' being trained in college and university programs, Unger has a very strong point of view. A graduate himself of NYU, which has one of the country's leading film programs, Unger feels that it is inappropriate for film programs to attempt to train technicians, although he is strongly supportive of the schools' intellectual efforts—training writers, producers, and directors. When it comes to skills like camera and sound, Unger feels that the college experience is a long way from the realities of working professionally. He points to the recent graduate who knows how to turn on a NAGRA sound recorder and describes himself as being "able to take sound." As for the straight technical jobs like grips or gaffers, Unger believes that colleges don't know how to train these people to meet the demands of the market and that the students are simply throwing their money away trying to get this background at a college or university.

Better, he reasons, for students interested in these areas to go out into the real world and begin apprenticeships. The years they would otherwise have spent in college can more fruitfully be spent making headway on a career.

In Unger's experience, this is part of a larger problem. College-trained students emerge into the workplace and begin at the lowest level of "grunt" work. Unger has observed a very high burnout rate among them, owing principally to the frustrations experienced in the first few years of employment. Having made student films, they are convinced that their big break as a director or a cinematographer is just around the corner. The reality of the marketplace frequently catches them off guard. Unable to adapt to a rough blue-collar existence when they see themselves as artists or filmmakers, they leave the business in favor of other callings. For Unger, then, this is something of a self-fulfilling prophecy. The colleges have built an unreal level of expectation in their graduates, whose high hopes are dashed, causing many simply to abandon their film dreams and aspirations in favor of some other career.

As Unger casts a wary eye toward the future, he believes technology will facilitate new programming demands from a variety of new sources. Whether it be video or film, there will be an increasing demand for product and this will be good for labor. He acknowledges that some of the present jurisdictional boundaries may be obsolete in a new market but feels that the overall impact will be a favorable one. Unger is unwilling to separate the film business and its present difficulties from the rest of the economy. Where labor stands in an overall sense, he believes, there stands this part of the film industry. The larger state of the national economy and various major market forces and pressures will all be felt in the motion picture industry. In short, just as the movie business discovered during the Great Depression, it is impossible to separate the motion picture business from what is happening all around it. Its product may be the stuff that dreams are made of, but its problems are only too real.

Unger recognizes that no matter what kind of a picture he paints of the movie business, the passion in many people will be unquenchable. Those individuals will not be deterred by the fact that most of the union locals across the country have more qualified workers than there are jobs in which to place them. He knows that this fact alone will not keep the gifted, the persistent, and the passionate from continuing to try to win places for themselves in the industry. To those newcomers, Unger says, "Get in and get started. Sweep the floors, if necessary, but get in the door and start to work."

The advice is sound. Begin wherever you can and bring your dedication with you. No position need last forever. Build from one position to the next, impressing all your fellow workers at every step along the way. The thought to keep in mind is that some people are going to make it, and you might as well be one. Your talents and your dedication will allow you to get through the difficult times and keep moving closer to your goal. Others have done it offering far less than you have to offer. Above all else, keep the flame of your passion for film burning bright. It will always light the way for you and permit you to grow and prosper.

THE STUDIO: PRODUCTION AND CORPORATE

Perhaps there is no more representative symbol of the picture business than the motion picture studio. A creation of the earliest days of the movie industry, the studios came to stand for those business entities that maintained both production facilities and distribution or marketing capabilities. While fashions have changed in the picture industry, the concept of a studio supporting a production and a marketing capability has continued to this day.

Studios are considerably less than efficient, well-oiled business machines. Their excesses and idiosyncrasies have been exhaustively detailed in the popular press. Much of the criticism directed at them is well deserved. The trappings of studio positions are unparalleled from the standpoint of luxury and creature comforts. Office furnishings, foreign cars, expense accounts, and, in recent years, salaries and other emoluments all exist on a grand scale that is the envy of most other corporate executives. On the negative side—and there is a negative side—there is no job security beyond the length of one's employment contract, the work is certain to consume weekends and evenings, and there is very little existence outside of business contacts. This can put terrible pressure on one's domestic situation. Evenings out are usually dedicated to business dinners at trendy restaurants. Even vacations are often spent with business associates and their spouses. Hollywood is a town built on personal contacts, and few players in the movie game let any time slip by without pursuing these relationships.

Yet the glamour and power of the studio find few comparisons with the possible exception of the world of politics. Not surprisingly, those seeking satisfaction in politics have enjoyed close ties over the years with those in Hollywood. The personality types drawn to the two professions are very similar. Even the appearance of power—never mind the real thing—can be very seductive and inwardly satisfying. The studio, with its ultimate power to create, distribute, and market a film, can furnish that opportunity to its executives.

The production side of a studio is organized in a vertical fashion resembling the typical pyramid arrangement found in many businesses. At the bottom of the pyramid, and enjoying a curious kind of power unique to motion pictures, are the readers. These individuals "cover" the 100–150 submissions made to the studio each week. These submissions come in the form of screenplays, books, plays, articles, treatments, ideas, songs—almost any form of intellectual property that can be adapted into a motion picture. Since no one person could possibly read all of this material, the job of the reader is to prepare a one-to two-page synopsis of the submission, followed by his recommendation as to what action the studio should take. The reader's power lies in the fact that if he dislikes the material, in almost every case the studio will pass on it and return it to the submitter without further examination. If the reader supports the material, it will usually be read by one or more production executives to determine what further action should be taken. Good readers are essential to the operation of a studio. Not only must they be able to recognize quality when they see it, but they must also have the creative ability to suggest how promising work can be made better. They should be on the cutting edge of the marketplace, both in identifying the exciting members of the creative community and in anticipating the shifting tides of public taste.

Some studios have unionized their readers, making them keep regular hours at the studio and work for set hourly rates. Other studios treat readers as free-lance workers who simply pick up and drop off material once a week. These readers are paid by the number of pieces they cover, with one price applying to screenplays, another to novels, and so on. To become a union reader, you must work thirty days for a signatory company. These companies will select their readers from the Producers' Roster. When times are slow, as they were in 1991–1992, there could be as many as fifty union readers out of work. This makes admission to the union difficult. In better times, all available union readers may be employed and admission to the union may not be as difficult to achieve. Even in hard times, if a studio wants an individual badly enough, it will find a way to hire him.

The free-lance reader position is greatly favored by many seeking to break into the movie business, especially beginning screenwriters. The position has the obvious advantages of being able to work on one's own time, providing some contact with people in the industry, and allowing one to stay familiar with the kind of material that is in the marketplace.

The reader position, in most cases, is a dead-end job. There is no effort to promote readers to higher levels at the studio unless the reader demonstrates singular abilities. In my experience as a studio executive, I discovered that too often readers would try to make a favorable impression by staunchly supporting the best submission they had read that week. While that may be understandable in terms of human nature, it tends to put more work in front of already overworked studio personnel. To curb that tendency, I'd call all the readers in on Monday mornings to meet with the creative executives, where they were asked to defend at length any property that had earned their endorsement the previous week. This step not only brought the desired selectivity back into the system, but tended to identify who the most perceptive readers were. In fact, that process caused one of the readers to be elevated to an executive position that served as his springboard to a successful career in the business.

Rates for covering material will vary depending on the studio and the pay scale. You can expect around $50–$75 for reading and covering a screenplay, and twice that, or more, for a novel. Depending on the quantity of submissions and the number of readers employed, an average reader assignment may be five to six pieces a week. Reading material is certainly not a job for those seeking a fast fix to their economic predicament. It may, however, be more constructive and conducive to furthering a career than would waiting on tables or driving a limousine or teaching aerobics classes.

To secure a reading position at the studios, you should either pursue the union local, #554, 13949 Ventura Boulevard, Suite 301, Sherman Oaks, California, (818) 784-6555, or seek a tryout with any studio employing nonunion readers. Most tryouts consist of writing up coverage on a screenplay with which the studio is already familiar. Your work will be held up to existing thinking about the property in question and will be judged accordingly. How clearly you can express yourself in simple declarative sentences, and how insightful your recommendation is, will be the major criteria used to measure the acceptability of your work. If you are able to bring humor or style to your recommendation, so much the better. First and foremost, however, your taste must reflect objective quality standards, and your judgments must be tempered by an understanding of the reality of the marketplace. As there is considerable movement among those holding reader jobs, it is a good idea to stay in touch with any contacts that you are able to make in the reading community. Sometimes other readers hear about openings, while at other times, supportive executives will be able to keep your name in active circulation.

Coordinating the actions of the readers at most studios is the story editor. Absent unusual qualifications, this would not be an entry-level position. It is a job that goes to former readers, people from the world of book publishing, or others with contacts in the writing community. In earlier times, the job of story editor was a position of some importance in the studio firmament. Armed with a wide literary background and the skills to make a promising screenplay into a great one, the story editor worked closely with screenwriters, much like their counterpart editors in the world of publishing. They maintained close working relationships with established writers, kept a watch out for new talented writers, and played an important part in the operation of the studio.

Gradually, the position slipped into being one of details and administrative functions. Today's story editor assigns the readers their material, keeps current lists of credits and availabilities, and makes suggestions to the production executives of writers for specific projects. Sometimes they are asked to write memorandums detailing how scripts, especially those commissioned by the studio, can be improved in the next draft. On rare occasions, they are actually permitted to meet directly with the writer, frequently as part of a larger meeting with a production executive. In previous times, writers maintained close friendships and symbiotic working relationships with the story editors in a studio. Now writers maintain those relationships with the more powerful production executives. This may be very positive in terms of furthering their careers, but it rarely does any good for the quality of their writing.

To be sure, in earlier times the writers were under contract to the studio, rather than working as writers for hire as they do today. Still, the story editor had vastly different responsibilities then compared with today.

In an odd way, the lessening of the importance of the story editor was furthered by the feminist movement that burst upon the scene in the 1960s and 1970s. By that time, most of the studios were using women as story editors, paying them too little and using them as resources away from the action of production. These women tended to be ambitious, talented, and keenly deserving of more responsibility and more compensation. When their voices of protest were added to those of women in other professions, the studios finally relaxed some of their gender constraints and began to allow women into the ranks of the production executives and even higher in the corporate world. With the departure of this group of story editors—many of whom had enjoyed very successful careers in publishing—the story editor ranks were thinned even more. Today, the position is a mere vestige of what it used to be years ago.

The job that women wanted access to, and the position that

holds most of the allure in studio life, is that of production executive. Variously known as production vice presidents, creative affairs executives, or other similar designations, these individuals all perform similar tasks. They are responsible for attracting viable film projects to the studio, shepherding them through the development period, and supervising their production as motion pictures. When the answer print is finally completed—that is, when the movie is finished and prints have been struck for distribution to theaters—the production executives turn it over to the marketing department of the studio to sell. Competition among the studios is intense for the best projects, and good relationships with actors, directors, and writers are considered a prime asset in this position. In today's Hollywood, where talent agents control so much of the disposition of material and packages, the relationship issue extends with equal weight to the elite agents plying their trade in New York and Los Angeles.

While fundamentally production executives do the same thing whatever their titles, there is a big difference in the ability they have to say yes to creative and business decisions. Can they approve a development deal? And to what dollar limit? Can they approve a picture commitment, and if so, to what dollar limit? Can they approve actors or directors for a given project? These are the kinds of concerns that people inside and outside the studio have about production executives. Sometimes this information is hard to ferret out. It may also be changeable depending on the economic climate at the studio or in the country. Suffice it to say that production executives function with different degrees of corporate responsibility, although the limits may not be the easiest thing to discern.

Since the days when the studios had all their creative talent under contract are gone, it has become more and more difficult to put together the right creative elements for a motion picture. Ironically, this change has occurred during periods where the average cost of a motion picture has escalated dramatically, along with the associated risks. Many are the properties that have languished in development hell, unable to attract the actor or the director that the studio deems necessary to make them viable. So, naturally, there is a premium on production executives whose contacts and relationships facilitate getting pictures made. They are compensated very handsomely for these skills. The difficulty, of course, is that a good package does not a successful movie make. Too little time and attention is focused on the more important problem of improving the script. Moreover, the present crop of studio executives are not as skilled in this area as they are in maintaining relationships. Only prohibitive costs have sporadically deterred the studios from their conviction that if big stars want to do a project, it must be a project worth doing.

It can never be forgotten that audiences don't go to movies because of the dazzling ingenuity of the deals that set the creative team in place. They may be attracted by the stars, or even the director, but ultimately the success of the film will be measured by the satisfaction of the audience and the subsequent word-of-mouth enthusiasm that it engenders. More than anything else, this will hinge on how well the audience responded to the story being told. The principal problem with movies today is that their overseers are better versed in the art of making deals and maintaining relationships than they are in developing worthy scripts and making good movies.

While it is possible to find some kind of entry-level job in the production area of a studio, most executives come from the ranks of agents or motion picture producers. They hold these studio positions for a period of time and then drift to another studio, or perhaps back to agency or producing work. Maybe they distinguished themselves, maybe the administration they worked for simply changed, and as in politics, a new team was put in place. Usually success as a production executive is measured by the number of hit films with which you are associated. It is easy to play it safe and not become too closely associated with any project. In so doing, it is perhaps possible to avoid the risks of failed films. Most executives prefer to support one or more projects actively in the hope that they can ride the coattails of the film's successes. To be the executive who fought hard for a controversial film that finally got made and became a big success is the best way to distinguish yourself in this area of the industry.

It is also the fastest route to become the chief production executive, known in the parlance of the business as the head of production. With today's proliferation of executive titles, this job may be known as the president or the chairman of the motion picture division. It remains the desk where the buck stops. The production head must ultimately take credit or blame for the slate of films that the studio produces. Disasters or hits, he must live in the limelight and wrestle with the critics, the money people, the creative community, and the supporting players like agents and lawyers who work for them. The other production executives take their proposals to him, and his is the final word on the subject. Lavishly paid and provided for, his job is notoriously short-lived. It is not uncommon for him to be removed from it even before the films he has commissioned have been released. Three women, Sherry Lansing, Paula Weinstein, and Dawn Steele, have acceded to this position at different studios, and the assumption has to be that it is now available to women and men alike.

It is all well and good to speak of high-powered executives with their seven-figure salaries and bonuses and other perks, but what of the individual seeking a foothold in the studio world? Where should he turn, and what kinds of slots might be available for someone with no experience? Entry-level jobs, even though they pay very little, are as dependent on the overall economy as executive positions. When things are tough, as they are at this writing, many studios, like other businesses, impose a hiring freeze and elect to stay with their existing personnel. Indeed, they suddenly find that they are able to do without many of those they previously had believed were virtually indispensable. This kind of thinking throws a decided damper on the plans of many ambitious young people desiring a chance to prove themselves in motion pictures. This industry is cyclical, however. Today's bad times will inevitably give way to rosier times at some point in the future. The industry has functioned in such fashion since it burst upon the scene nearly 100 years ago, and there is no reason to suspect that it will do otherwise in the future.

As the film industry faced various crises, many people have predicted that it was finished as a viable economic force in America and the world. Whether the obstacle was a depression, war, the gas crunch, the advent of television or videocassettes, or simply bad films, the industry has always weathered the storm and come back even stronger. There doesn't appear to be anything on the horizon that would change the inherent resilience of the motion picture business. Timing is always problematic. There are many factors outside motion pictures that have to be considered to determine when an uptick might occur. Whenever it does, there are certain moves that might be taken to try to get onto a studio payroll.

The first of these may not produce any income whatsoever. That is an area of the business known as internships. Sometimes paying, but more often not, internships are created by the studio for the dual purpose of training future employees and getting free labor. Whatever your opinion of the morality of free labor, if you can afford to work for a period without compensation, an internship is an excellent way to get your foot into the studio door. You may find yourself in some phase of the literary area of the studio, or in production. It is not overly important. You will be on the lot, part of the team, and therefore able to gain access to people who were only names to you before. You will know first about openings, who to see to try to fill the available slot, and what the prospects for movement within the studio might be. None of those benefits would be available to someone not working at the studio.

Any entry-level job is only a chance, an opportunity to meet and impress people and move up in the organization. Typically, there will be other young people working shoulder to shoulder with you, sharing the same dreams and aspirations. Probably not everyone will be asked to stay on. Some will be asked to leave. This is unavoidable, as nothing is guaranteed to you in the workplace. All you can realistically hope for is a chance to show someone what you can do and who you are. Internships provide you that opportunity.

In the previous discussion of studio personnel, the jobs of readers and production executives were touched upon. There is nothing easy about landing either of these positions. You may need to pull out all the stops just to get to see someone at a studio, never mind getting hired. What you should remember, however, is that others before you have successfully ventured down this path. And they have made it. Why, then, can't you? Confidence, bravado, even egotism, are all traits that characterize many individuals in the picture business. They do not suggest character flaws or weaknesses as much as they indicate someone likely to be successful in this line of work. It is important to keep this in mind when you have an opportunity to sit down across the desk from someone in the studio world.

Another kind of entry-level position that has earned major dividends for those who have secured it is the job of executive assistant. Often, there isn't such a position in existence. It may fall to you to convince someone that he can't possibly do without your assistance for one more day. If you are successful with your arguments, you are likely to find yourself keeping notes or performing like functions for a major power broker in the studio firmament.

You don't secure an executive assistant position by writing to the personnel director of a studio. Personnel will be quick to respond that no such position exists. Instead, your letter should be directed to specific executives at specific studios. Unless your letter is remarkable in some respect, in most cases you won't even be given the courtesy of a reply. Your résumé, in all probability, is not going to be appreciably different from those of hundreds of other job seekers. Maybe you were a film major in college, maybe you have a graduate degree of some kind, maybe you even have some job experience in a related or unrelated field. None of these credits is sufficient to cause people to jump up and down over your application. In some fashion, your cover letter has to call attention to you and separate you from all the rest of the qualified people seeking employment. Your letter must demonstrate what you can do for the person to whom you are writing and why you, uniquely, can do it.

It would be helpful when you write this letter, and imperative should you be given an interview, to find out as much as you possibly can about the company and the individual to whom you are writing. Years ago, trying to escape from a law firm in New York where I was working, I wrote such a letter to a variety of high-placed executives in New York. I got a favorable response from John Kluge, then head of Metromedia and now one of the country's most successful and wealthiest executives. Arriving at the appointed hour at his office, I was asked very pointedly what I could do for him to make his life a better one. I had done no research on his business, didn't really know what his day consisted of or where his problems lay. My general answers were far from persuasive to him, and in short order I was thanked for my interest and shown the door. Case in point. I blew that chance to go to work for a dynamic, high-powered executive by not taking the time to research the situation thoroughly. Whatever I said in my letter to him apparently sparked his interest, but from there, my experience was nothing short of disastrous. There are no shortcuts in this game. You have to do the work and the preparation necessary to make an impression and give yourself a fighting chance to secure the post you want.

Should you be fortunate enough to land an executive assistant position, know that you have found an exceptional opportunity to learn and to propel yourself forward. The job will take enormous dedication and commitment, often running far into the evening and weekends. The parameters will probably be as broad as you want them to be. Most busy executives will discover that an assistant is so invaluable that they don't understand how they ever did without one. But to be effective at that kind of job, you have to vacuum up work going far beyond ordinary office duties. Reading scripts, writing memorandums, even dropping things off at the dry cleaner's—all are fair game. There will be more than ample rewards down the road that arise out of this kind of commitment. If you are fortunate enough to secure a position like this, make the most of it and don't mess up a unique opportunity.

The studio is a big concern. As such, it has other departments in addition to the production area. One such department is concerned with the physical production of the films put out by the studio. Often known only to those who actually make a film for the studio, these hardworking individuals ride herd on the budgets of the studio films. Most have practical experience actually making films (something that many of their more publicized production colleagues do not).

Functioning in this area of the studio are production executives who prepare the budgets for the films to be shot. They are skilled production manager types who can call upon their own vast production experience as well as troubleshoot problems as they occur. In addition, there are other specialists who oversee everything from postproduction deals to sound to music. In many cases, the sound business judgments of these people are overruled by the production executives who are closer to the creative talent and have the authority to approve overages when persuaded that a better film will result. There is little doubt that if the physical production people reigned supreme, instead of their creative production brethren, the excesses of over-budget spending would be largely a thing of the past.

This area of a studio is a no-frills operation. Relationships are not deemed important, and thus unlimited expense accounts and expensive foreign cars do not come with the job. These individuals are no less hardworking, however. They are called upon to render overnight budget guesstimates, asked to fly off to remote locations at a moment's notice, and generally entrusted with the conservation of the studio's dollars in all stages of the production process. Anyone dealing with the spending of discretionary money knows that it is always easy to say no. The more difficult task these people face is to balance the equities, fall back on experience, have sufficient command of all of the facts, and then render a decision. The top production people in Hollywood are far from studio yes-men. They effectively straddle the line between the studio to which their loyalty must ultimately lie and the needs of the production. In most cases, the relationship between the physical production people and the production team is not adversarial. Out of an understanding of the problems that a production faces can come help and support.

Most physical production departments do not have a formal system in place to hire interns or those seeking entry-level positions. As with any spot in the picture business, it is very helpful to know the people involved, or at least have an introduction to them. For the individual seeking to find a niche in this area of the business, there is nothing to lose by mounting a strong offensive at a number of studios and trying to secure some kind of position. One thing to remember about the business: it is a very small operation. Even if you are unsuccessful in getting the position you want this time, you may be able to leave a good impression with someone that will pay dividends for you sometime in the future. It is often difficult to think of your life in other than immediate terms. Rent and bills have to be paid now. Tomorrow is another question entirely. Yet motion pictures is a business of personal contacts. The more contacts you can make, and the more favorable impressions you can create, the better the foundation you build for the rest of your professional life.

In addition to producing and marketing films, the studio is a corporation with all the needs that corporations have. It is likely that you will find housed in a studio such varied departments as business affairs, legal, casting, public relations, and finance. Depending on your background and your ultimate aspirations, one of these departments may be a perfect segue for you. If you have a law degree, for example, and have worked for an entertainment firm long enough to know that your heart lies not in the practice of law but in the movie business, a studio's legal department may be an appropriate stepping-stone for you. My personal exodus from the law came through such a progression. I left a Manhattan law firm to become the attorney for a talent agency. Within two years, I had become an agent and left the agency to head production at a New York–based studio. It doesn't always happen with that rapidity, but you have to be in the game. You have to put yourself in a position where your goal can be a realistic possibility, and not simply an idle dream.

There are risks—but life is full of risks. The legal or business affairs chief at a studio certainly does not view his department as a stepping-stone to the more glamorous side of the studio. It is safe to predict that he will have no interest in hiring someone he thinks is taking a position only to get out at the earliest opportunity. But no one signs lifetime commitments. You go to work in good faith and what happens, happens.

As in the physical production department of the studio, most of the corporate studio positions parallel those in businesses outside the studio. To a certain extent, there is a revolving-door quality to these positions as the same people are encountered no matter which side of the desk they happen to be occupying that particular moment. The entertainment attorney working at a studio deals with the same attorneys, agents, and business managers that he encountered in private practice. Likewise, the casting director for a studio must deal with the same agents and personal managers that he would encounter if he were working on his own. Again, it is a remarkably small universe and the key is to get your foot in the door and become a player. You may not, and probably won't, obtain your dream position with your entry-level job, but if you have breached the walls of the studio and found some situation, you are on your way.

Such departments as legal, business affairs, and casting are really support areas for the production department. They are empowered to make suggestions, but rarely to make policy. Thus, the casting director will furnish the creative executives lists of talent for the key roles in a film to be produced, but the final decision will come from other quarters. Similarly, when an attorney for the studio reports that he is at loggerheads with an agent over a deal for an important star, his position can be overridden by the executive trying to make that picture a reality. This suggests again the premium placed on power or control in Hollywood. It lends further weight to the motivation of many of the support personnel in a studio to move laterally to a position where they will have more of the final say on matters from casting to budget to policy.

Areas such as finance or public relations are not dissimilar to comparable areas outside the studio. Public relations work does not differ dramatically whether you have your own shop or are employed by a studio. These are corporate positions with all the pluses and minuses that suggests. You get paid regularly, have your share of the perks that come to corporate employees, but are a small player in a large cast of characters. For some, this is an ideal environment. For others, it is a means to get to another end.

Studios do not recruit personnel on college campuses in the manner of other large corporations. In part, this arises out of the fact that there is never a shortage of people seeking to work in a studio environment. There are always more people who want positions than there are positions to fill. Securing an entry-level spot is a matter of perseverance, good timing, and often luck. As Aesop said, "The gods help them that help themselves." There is much that can be done to influence studios to treat your application favorably. Do not hesitate to call upon all of your contacts to try to bring about the desired result. In most cases, all such intervention will only get you a meeting. The rest is up to you. Realistically, that is all you can expect. If you are provided an opportunity to strut your stuff, seize the moment and convince them that you are the right person for the job. If you dedicate yourself to it with all your energy and talent, the chances are you *are* that person.

THE MOVIE BUSINESS: THE MARKETING SIDE OF THE STUDIO

From the time the major companies took shape, to today's motion picture environment, the movie business has really been two and sometimes three businesses. A studio is first involved in the production of motion pictures. Working in development to make properties into screenplays, to bring directors and cast to the screenplays, and to attract sufficient capital to fashion well-made movies, the studios have dominated the American movie scene since early in this century.

Their second business has been the distribution of these films. At first this just entailed getting the movies into the theaters. Now it includes not only theatrical distribution but also videocassettes and laser discs, pay and cable, television and non-theatrical distribution. This has become, in today's marketplace, a global business in which revenues from outside the United States (and Canada) are roughly the equal of domestic revenue.

Periodically, the government has seen fit to permit the distribution companies (the studios) to own and manage motion picture theaters. At times when this was permitted, such as now, the studios have also found themselves in the exhibition business, with all its benefits and its problems.

If exhibition is easily severable as a basic business of the studios, the business of marketing or distribution is not. The marketer must build public awareness of films, create a strong "want-to-see" reaction and negotiate terms that are as favorable as possible for the studio's interest. For a studio to succeed, it must have in place a team of talented men and women who can maximize the potential grosses, from all sources, throughout the world, of the very expensive films they have produced and/or financed. Under the marketing rubric, there are, in fact, two separate businesses that make up the studios' operations. These businesses serve the two principal demands of a consumer-oriented product—advertising/publicity and sales.

The advertising and publicity people are charged with formulating a marketing strategy for the films, including doing the research necessary to guide the company in its decision making. With these concerns comes the creation of advertising materials to create public awareness about the forthcoming films and to persuade the public to see them. These marketing efforts carry a large price tag in today's marketplace. The average studio picture, by way of example, currently incurs costs in excess of $11 million for its prints and its advertising. Most of that money is channeled into newspaper, magazine, radio, and TV advertising—the media buy—to support the films at the time they are distributed. The price of television time, network or local, is considered cost-efficient and highly effective, notwithstanding its high price. Even the special-interest films from small distributors must look to $3–$4 million in prints and advertising if they are to gain any acceptance in the marketplace. The irony exists that many of these independent films will cost far more to market than they did to produce. But such is the nature of the problem in trying to make some portion of the American audience aware of a film and desirous of seeing it. So costly is the marketing effort that one wag suggested that the greatest boon for the picture business would be if the government prohibited it from advertising on television.

Fred Goldberg, industry marketing veteran, characterizes the history of motion picture distribution in his definitive book, *Motion Picture Marketing and Distribution* (Focal Press, 1991). He argues that in earlier times the distribution (sales) side of the business coexisted with the advertising, publicity, and promotion side, whereas today distribution is in the ascendancy. Typically, the head advertising person reports to the head of distribution. This has tended to resolve the classic disagreements between operating divisions where the sales people would fault the materials and ad campaigns for the films and the marketing people would take exception to the way the film was booked, or licensed to the theaters. (Both could always agree, however, that they would have made very different choices about which films should be produced.) Today, distiibution doesn't resemble the old methods of booking films very closely. Movies no longer play off in different runs at different quality theaters. The window of theatrical distribution is much shorter than previously so as to allow the subsequent distribution windows of pay/cable, videocassette, and syndicated (or network) television to open up sooner. Films will open on more screens (2,300 is not an unusual number), so as to maximize the cost-effectiveness of the advertising dollar.

From an economic standpoint, this has reduced the way domestic distribution is carried out. No longer are 10,000 play dates commonplace over the run of a picture. Now a film will open in 1,000 to 2,500 situations and add another 1,000 dates before it moves along to other distribution opportunities. This change in how domestic distribution is carried out has affected the nature of how the distribution companies choose to align themselves. In prior times, as many as thirty exchanges, spread throughout the country, handled the distribution business for the studios. Nowadays, the number of branches has shrunk to around six in most of the major companies. The rise in importance in ancillary rights, especially pay/cable and videocassette, is principally responsible for these changes.

Yet as much as the business shifts with the varying tides of audience preferences, still it stays basically the same. The job of the marketer is still to get people into the theater seats. When the business pauses to look at itself, as it is doing at this writing, the emphasis in terms of stars and directors is always on that handful of personalities who can legitimately "open" a picture. It is a rare thing indeed to fill the seats on opening night simply because a specific actor is included in the cast. In the world of high finance that the picture business has become, that ability is rewarded handsomely. With that high degree of public acceptance, however, also comes the galvanized effort of the marketing end of the distribution company. Their strategy for marketing will have begun at the time of production, if not before. They will have plugged the film into the yearly schedule for distribution, and if a peak season such as Christmas or summer is involved, they will probably have already booked the film, sight unseen. The marketing strategy will continue through preproduction as the unit publicist and the unit photographer create the tools that will accompany the selling of the picture. Often a special photographer will be employed to shoot and place pictures taken during production in domestic and foreign periodicals and newspapers. Research will also be undertaken to assist in discovering the marketing problems for the film. For example, Warner Bros., in researching the highly touted release of *Superman,* discovered that the public felt the flying had to be believable if the film was to work. Director Richard Donner and the entire production team spent many hours accomplishing this on film, and the ultimate box office results speak for themselves.

Other research will be conducted from the time of production through the release of the picture. The function of research is theoretically to bring the voice of the consumer to the table. While the concept is certainly sound, in practice the research conducted in the picture business is less than objective and instead, generally serves as reinforcement for already established marketing philosophies of the distribution company. It is paid for by the distribution company and is generally employed to underscore the wisdom of corporate thinking to the filmmakers involved with the project. Certainly, with the larger pictures the number of interviews rises dramatically and the database becomes somewhat more reliable. The smaller the number of interviews, however, the less reliable the data, no matter what the studio puts out as gospel.

Research has attained tremendous importance in recent years. In the past, old-line film marketers were far more inclined to do their own research by seat-of-the-pants techniques. From Columbia Pictures founder Harry Cohn's famous proclamation about judging audience reactions by paying attention to restlessness in the theater, to the then-common practice of marketing people visiting several theaters where their films were playing, the sense of knowledge by personal observation was the basis for most movie research. Today, most distribution companies spend an average of $300,000 on the accumulation of research data for each film they release. Rarely will that research be an instrument for changing already set corporate thinking.

The campaign selected by the marketing personnel must embody persuasive posters or one-sheets, preferably ones that can reduce in size for newspaper advertising, trailers, television spots, radio spots, videocassette press kits, and other forms of sales and distribution aids. All of these advertising materials, from poster art to copy lines, should be built upon a single marketing strategy. They should work together to convey a single impression to a specific audience segment so that members of that audience segment will feel they have to see the movie.

If done correctly, the company will have identified the target audience for the film accurately. It will proceed to aim all its materials at that audience segment. The more precise the studio can be in identifying the target audience for a film, the better the chance the film will succeed theatrically. The business is full of horror stories concerning missed opportunities arising out of the studio's failure to identify the basic audience for a film. Sometimes simple demographics are not enough. Audiences tend to like what they like, research notwithstanding. Films like *Driving Miss Daisy* and *Fried Green Tomatoes* greatly exceeded what studio research felt they would generate at the box office. It is a big country and motion picture research is an inexact science. Audiences will have the last word. The immortal words of screenwriter William Goldman operate in this sphere, as they do in production: "Nobody knows anything."

If market research for a given film presents serious credibility problems, at least the database for results of all prior film releases is now in place. This allows a distribution company to assess a given genre of film in terms of what time of year it opens, how similar films have performed, how it performs in certain key situations, against strong, medium, or weak competition, and what the anticipated falloff in weekly business should amount to at different times of the year. Having this information stored in the computer allows models to be constructed that have proven very useful to the distribution end of the business. There is nothing speculative or self-serving about this kind of research. Instead, it is a critical tool now employed by all distributors to assist them in planning and marshaling their assets so as to maximize the profits on their films.

One thing is certain. The surest route to disaster at the box office is to fail to target the correct audience for a film. Had a film like *Bull Durham* been perceived as a baseball picture and not as a sophisticated, sexy comedy, there is little doubt that the box office grosses would have been a fraction of what they turned out to be. The marketing executives must be careful not to cast their audience nets too widely. In the competition for the consumer's leisure time dollar (or, more correctly, $7.50), the winning entry will usually be the best film coupled with the campaign that alerts the appropriate audience to that film's existence.

Often overlooked by the outsider who sees constant evidence of the amounts of money spent in advertising is the effort the distributor puts into publicity and promotion. This task will have begun even before production, intensified during production, and peaked during the release of the film. It will include promotional films, press kits and publicity stills, promotions, music videos, screenings, junkets, personal appearance tours, giveaways, and TV clips. The ubiquitous movie star plugging his latest film on late-night or morning talk shows is but one highly visible example of these activities. Such publicity and promotion activities are seen as a complement to the advertising expenditures and not as replacements for them.

At the other center of distribution activity are the executive and staff that compose what used to be referred to as the sales department. For them, the country is divided into four sections, Eastern, Western, Central, and Southern. Job responsibilities may be broken down further, with certain executives charged only with booking and servicing the New York market, or with handling print control or similar tasks. The physical handling, servicing, and shipment of prints could one day be a dated practice. Much has been written and speculated about the movie business going toward down-link viewing on large-screen HDTV presentations that would render 35mm prints and their associated problems of shipping and handling obsolete. While anyone who has carried 35mm film cans any distance will wish that day were upon us, there is no indication that it is imminent.

The distribution personnel of a studio are generally not involved with the "sale" of their product. (One important exception to this is in the videocassette industry.) Theatrically, and in television distribution, films are rented or licensed for exhibition. This is done pursuant to a negotiated contract between the distribution company and the theater chain or other outlet seeking to exhibit the film in question. Many economic terms, from division of box office receipts to exhibitor guarantees to length of term to exclusivity, must be covered in these agreements. Typically, they are based on certain assumptions of the film's popularity with the audience. These expectations can be a long way off the mark, which will necessitate subsequent renegotiations between the parties. The process is an ongoing one and always full of some measure of rancor. The truth is that, despite the perennial grousing, both sides need each other and will probably continue in the fashion they have grown accustomed to over time. Exhibitors will continue to balk at the large guarantees demanded and distributors will continue to assert some right to a percentage of the revenue derived from the concession business, which the exhibitor jealously husbands for himself. Over the years, the gross abuses of the process such as block booking (forcing the exhibitor to take all films if he is to get the most popular) and blind bidding (forcing the exhibitor to bid on films he has not viewed) have tended to be scorned and prohibited as common practices.

With all the data accumulated over all the years that films have been shown to the public, distribution remains an inexact science. When a film should be released, in how many theaters, with what kind of campaign, and to what target audience, remain questions that have to be answered anew for each film released by a distribution company. Comparing the process to other forms of consumer product marketing, several differences emerge. First, the marketplace for films is highly dynamic. A film can become the country's "favorite" film in its first weekend of release. Second, the audience tends to make up its mind instantaneously and rarely can the distribution companies get the audience to change its collective mind. Finally, unlike most other consumer-oriented products, one rarely knows the quality of the competitors' products. That is, if a distributor is preparing a major summer release, it will know the title and creative elements in its competitors' films, but will not know the answer to the critical question of whether the films are any good. These uncertainties put great pressure on the distribution executives and probably account for the inherent difficulty the industry has in adequately handling special films that don't have familiar antecedents. While this is lamentable, it is certainly understandable in light of the history of the business.

In speaking with past and present marketers and distribution executives, it becomes clear that there is no agreement as to a prescribed route to follow to succeed in this area of the motion picture industry. Fred Goldberg, who headed studio marketing operations for United Artists, Orion, and Columbia Pictures, found most success in hiring personnel by gravitating to business majors from the college ranks. As the business grew more sophisticated, he tended to seek prospective employees from those who graduated with M.B.A.'s. But above all else, Goldberg was drawn to those who evinced a genuine passion for movies. The business end of the movie industry is not easy. It never has been. The stakes are high and the players around the table are very talented. To succeed, in Goldberg's mind, it is imperative that one bring unbridled enthusiasm, or passion, to the job. Without it, he feels the prospective employee might better look elsewhere to find his niche in show business.

According to Goldberg, the foremost qualification for working in advertising/publicity is the ability to write well and to generate ideas. He asserts that there are myriad uses to which a good writer can be put in a marketing operation. Press kits, daily releases, copy lines—these and many other pieces of material are issued daily by a distributor to keep the fires of advertising and publicity well stoked. While to a degree these are acquired skills, there is little doubt that good writers will find a more welcome response in applying for entry-level positions than mediocre writers.

With respect to worthwhile activities that can legitimately be pursued before seeking employment with a distribution company, there is much that may prove useful down the road. Advertising agencies provide, even in intern or apprentice positions, a chance to work with copy and sales materials. The experience can be very analogous to motion picture work. Similarly, there is much benefit to be derived from working in the related field of exhibition—that is, working in an actual movie theater (see page 173). Experience at the point of sale will provide valuable lessons about the movie business. Such jobs, up to the level of theater manager, and even beyond, are readily available to the student seeking to intern or even put himself through school. Some colleges and universities are now offering courses in film marketing and distribution. Such training can jump-start a film career in this area by providing a solid background and perhaps even the contacts necessary to secure an entry-level industry position.

Fred Goldberg suggests, as has been observed previously, that care should be taken to write a dazzling cover letter to accompany your résumé. He and other executives insist they read all such job requests and could be swayed by an aggressive and creative letter. In addition, Goldberg is a strong proponent of taking advantage of *every* contact you might have to help secure a first position. No matter how far removed the contact person may seem, if you have access to him, take advantage of it. It always bears repeating that this is a "people business" and nothing has ever or will ever replace the benefits of personal recommendations. Everyone had to begin his career at some point. It is never a mistake to ask for help, a recommendation, an introduction, or the like. The worst that can happen is that you will be refused, and you will be no worse off for it. On the plus side, your whole career could take the direction you would like. The strategy should be clear. Reach out for help wherever you can. The strong likelihood is that it will be given and you will benefit from it. If not, nothing's lost.

A similar perspective to Fred Goldberg's is offered by Fred Mound, president of Universal Pictures Distribution. In keeping with motion picture tradition, he finds applicants with college educations more likely to be hired, but will consider those without degrees. In general, he seeks out more aggressive people for the sales positions that open up in his company. Selling is selling, no matter what the product line. A good salesman must have a streak of persuasiveness, whether it be called assertiveness, passion, or raw, undisguised aggression. Mound hopes to find the kind of outgoing personality that is effective in any marketplace to go along with the aforementioned aggressiveness.

At Universal, as with most major distribution companies, entry-level hires are placed in positions as sales trainees or general clerks. In a word, they are charged with learning the business. It behooves the new employee to pursue more than the scope of his everyday job. Keep asking questions; be nosy and find out the answers to problems you have; and exceed the expectations of your superiors. In the competitive world of film distribution, these rules are offered by the chief executives.

Mound hopes to recognize certain qualities that bode well

for success in those seeking entry-level positions in the marketing department of Universal. Creativity and imagination rank first on his list. Implicit within this observation is the fact that the most frequent target audience of moviegoers is the young—the fifteen- to twenty-five-year-olds. While film marketing does require voices of experience, those who have survived the rigors of unpredictable audience taste patterns, it also needs a constant replenishing with fresh, bright, and youthful talent. For this reason, Mound places a high value on finding young would-be marketers with strong creative instincts and talents. Significantly, he also looks for those with computer training. While computer sophistication came fairly late to the picture industry, it did nonetheless arrive. To be able to include a strong computer background on your résumé is something that can only increase your chances in a competitive job market.

As with nearly all of the jobs in Hollywood, recent years have seen significant breakthroughs in the hiring of women and minorities within the sales and marketing divisions of the studios. This is particularly true in the entry-level positions. At most companies, as with the creative side of the studios, the track record is stronger for women than for minorities. At different times, under different regimes, various Hollywood studios have been more aggressive about hiring and training minorities for all kinds of executive positions. These efforts have tended to be cyclical, more than part of an inexorable march to equality. Whether the opportunities offered minorities in front of the camera and on the set will translate to the business side of the industry is today an open question. Probably the best chance of this happening would be an infusion of bright and able minority newcomers at the base of the marketing pyramid. If their rise through the ranks coincided with the continuing public interest in films with minority actors and directors, then the next decade could be one of enormous positive change in the studio firmament.

The beginning pay at this end of the movie industry is consistent with most entry-level positions. Depending on education levels, skills, and the position involved, newcomers can look to make somewhere between $15,000 and $25,000 a year. There is reasonably quick upward salary movement from this figure, but there will also be a weeding out process. Some studios, such as Warner Bros., believe that in six months they can get an accurate sense of who can make it in that company and who can't. In the sales end for Warner Bros., for example, they will quickly move their up-and-coming executives into the field to the branch offices. If they continue to prosper, they can look forward to promotions to sales manager for a territory, then branch manager, and finally division manager. At Warner Bros., the compensation program is designed to reward a division manager with a base salary of around $125,000, with the opportunity to earn another $25–30,000 as a bonus. Intermediate positions would receive somewhat lesser amounts as executives worked their way up the corporate ladder.

As this discussion should be making clear, the business end of the movie industry may be a little sexier than most, but it remains a business. Hiring and advancement practices are not totally unlike those of other businesses throughout the country. Hard work and initiative, moreover, are as likely to be rewarded in this field as they are in any other. One thing to keep in mind about the business end of studio life: while the so-called creative side of the studio is firmly ensconced in Los Angeles, with skeletal offices in New York and perhaps London, the majority of people working in sales and marketing are located in the branches around the country. A sales job in Buffalo or Kansas City may not have the glamour that working in the studio in Burbank, or Universal City, or Century City has, but it is the all-important training ground for the future top executives. You should not expect to end up comfortably situated in the studio's home offices during your first years of employment for them.

It would be refreshing to be able to set down a surefire approach to breaking in to the sales or distribution sides of the studios. From a former top executive like Fred Goldberg to present top executives like Fred Mound and Barry Reardon of Warner Bros., the advice is always essentially the same. Some experience in sales, marketing, or even communication is better than none. It is well understood that someone just out of school will not have a résumé of overwhelming weight and importance. On the other hand, you may anticipate that your work record and experience will be carefully scrutinized. Such related experience as you've been able to accrue during your education will stand you in good stead.

This is especially important when it comes to a working knowledge of the picture business and its day-to-day operations. Reardon expressed his feelings that the more one knew about the business, the less likely he would end up disillusioned or burned out too early. Indeed, your investigations into the companies you are applying to should serve to reinforce your interest in the picture business in general. If that is not happening, you would be well advised to think about another line of work. There will always be positions to be filled, depending in part on the specific personnel then at a studio and on such outside factors as the state of the whole economy and the state of the movie business in particular. At this writing, for example, Fred Mound has a cautionary attitude regarding positions at Universal due to the downsizing currently a part of the Universal operation. Barry Reardon, speaking about the present atmosphere at Warner Bros., is decidedly more upbeat. He anticipates that there will be a relatively large turnover in the sales and marketing ranks, with many young people moving up with important promotions. It is thus incumbent on the aggressive job applicant to try to accumulate as much information as possible about the present shape of the distribution apparatuses of the studios. This is certainly easier to do in Los Angeles than in the country's heartland. Still, it is possible to glean information of this kind from trade stories in industry and other publications, from branch offices, or from networking with employees, agents, lawyers, vendors, filmmakers, and others who work in and around the motion picture world.

To a person, every executive in a position to hire young people stresses the importance of a cover letter to accompany your résumé. However you do this, your task is to separate your résumé from the rest of the stack by making yourself appear so unique and so talented that the executive simply *must* take the time to meet with you. It is a valuable chance for you to demonstrate how passionate and how creative you are. If addressed, as it should be, to the specific individual who heads up the marketing operation at the studio where you seek employment, the strong probability is that he will take the time to read it. Your cover letter and résumé are your first opportunity to show how well you can market and sell something—namely, yourself. Make it count! It may be the best chance you will have to wedge the door open wide enough for you to squeeze in.

At this writing, the future of the smaller distribution companies, such as Goldwyn and Miramax, is very much up in the air. In recent years, they have suffered the fate of many marginal businesses that did not come up with a big attraction that the public warmly embraced. Things seemed extraordinarily optimistic in the early 1980s when the first rush of videocassette deals seemingly promised the beginning of a healthy new era for the independents. As time went on, it became clearer that the videocassette business would finally be as difficult for the independents to prosper in as theatrical distribution, cable, and television were. Now is a time of consolidation and the mapping out of strategies for this decade. It stands to reason that some small distributors will survive this time and will grow and prosper. Which ones they will be is anything but clear.

Whichever direction the independents go, and whichever of them prove the survivors of the difficult times of the late 1980s and early 1990s, they will have to incorporate the computer database approach to marketing now in use by the majors. So long as the cost of marketing a large picture remains over $11.5 million, and even the marketing of a small, special-interest picture is running $3–4 million, then the importance of treating marketing with respect and with all the tools one can employ is self-evident. The companies must learn to adapt to more sophisticated methods and techniques and the employees of the future must learn to think in these terms. Such sophistication is long in coming and will probably be embraced more for defensive reasons than for long-term corporate strategies.

The tasks will remain a constant. Put customers in the theater seats and effect the best deals possible with the exhibitors so as to provide the most money for the distributors. The effective marketers and salespeople of tomorrow must have the skills to accomplish these ends.

THE SUPPORTING PLAYERS

The movie industry is shored up, wherever one looks, by an infrastructure of supporting players who, in a real sense, are responsible for facilitating much that takes place. Operating in ways that seem mysterious to outsiders, these individuals stand behind their more publicized clients in much the same way that politicians today have teams that strategize and carry out a variety of tasks for them. Sometimes compensated on an hourly basis, and sometimes on a percentage of their clients' earnings, the supporting players have risen to such prominence that in many instances they appear to have eclipsed the very clients they are paid to represent.

Included in a list of such people would be agents, attorneys, personal managers, business managers, publicists, and miscellaneous coaches and trainers. Some job categories are essential to the operation of the movie business, while others are more trendy, more an aspect of stardom or financial clout. For the individual looking seriously at working in a profession along these lines, it will be useful to have a better idea what these people do and what significance they have in the overall firmament.

Unquestionably the king of the jungle in today's Hollywood is the agent. Superagent Michael Ovitz of powerful Creative Artists Agency (CAA) is widely regarded as the single most powerful figure in Hollywood today. His power base includes not only the clients his agency represents, but also the major acquisitions he helps broker (the sale of Columbia and Universal Pictures to Japanese concerns), as well as such corporate marketing consultancies as the prestigious Coca-Cola account. Such representation is, however, more the exception than the rule. For the most part, agency representation follows more traditional lines.

An agent is employed to find work for his client, negotiate deals on his client's behalf, and advise his client as to the decisions that are in the best interest of building a career. The agent is compensated by 10 percent of the gross income the client receives, including any contingent compensation such as residuals or percentages of profits.

There are more than 300 agencies in Los Angeles, most of which are comparatively small boutique operations. Three large agencies, CAA, International Creative Management (ICM), and the William Morris Agency, are considered full-service agencies. As such, they have departments or agents handling everything from the legitimate stage to films, television, commercials, concerts, and book publishing. The larger agencies are vast information-gathering organizations that seek to stay on top of the actions of all the buyers of talent, material, and services, all over the world. Their client lists may run to many hundreds. While the smaller agencies may have one place of business in Los Angeles, the larger shops may have several offices throughout the country and in Europe.

The smaller agencies tend to specialize in one medium such as television or motion pictures, and define their sphere of activity still more by representing one kind of artist only. Thus, there are agencies representing only writers and directors, or editors, or composers, and so on. Their clients may be top people in their respective fields who choose to stay with a smaller shop rather than switch over to one of the larger agencies. Prevailing industry practice dictates that the large agencies refrain from stealing clients from the small agencies (but not refrain from stealing from each other).

Agencies are franchised by the various guilds as well as licensed by the state(s) in which they do business. This brings a considerable measure of legitimacy and respectability to their operations. There will always be a handful of unscrupulous, fly-by-night, peripheral people who hold themselves out as agents. In most instances, no matter what they claim, they have not been franchised by the guilds and are essentially operating illegally. A legitimate agency offers definite protections for its clients. Their exclusive representation may be terminated by the client if they are unsuccessful in bringing offers of work to the client in a prescribed period of time. Likewise, no legitimate agent is permitted, under Writers Guild of America policy, to charge anyone a reader's fee to look at a screenplay. These and other similar protections have grown out of prior abuses of the agency relationship. As a rule, industry practice and regulatory legislation have tended to eliminate these abuses.

In the picture business, the agents' ascension to power came in the late 1950s when the studios abandoned the contract system for talent. Until that time, writers, producers, directors, and actors were under term contracts with the studios and were paid a guaranteed yearly amount. When that system was abandoned, the agents rushed to fill the void, and the concept of the motion picture package was born. A package is two or more creative elements that have been combined by the agent and offered as a unit to a buyer. When the package contains, for example, a "hot" script, a major actor, and a major director, it may be irresistible to the studios. In putting such creative teams together, the agent thus performs a role that used to be solely the province of the studios. In former times, the executives at the studio had only to assign their contract talent to a picture and start the cameras rolling. Today, with the cost of motion pictures at record highs, it is far more difficult to attract the talent needed to "justify" the cost of the film. By controlling the talent, the agencies effectively control the process.

It is the agent's ability to put important elements together that causes multimillion-dollar performers to choose to pay out 10 percent of their income to an agent. Certainly Jodie Foster or Dustin Hoffman or Arnold Schwarzenegger would receive offers without an agent, and those offers could be more than adequately represented by the best lawyers that money could buy. Yet the access to the best material and the best creative elements is thought to come from an association with an important agency.

What makes a good agent? How does one gain access to this important area of the business? Agents are charged with *signing* clients, *selling* their services, and providing *career guidance.* Some agents are better at one of these tasks than another, but all successful agents have considerable competence at all of these skills. An agent is essentially a salesperson and will finally be judged by how successfully he sells the services of his clients. The job requires aggressive interpersonal skills since the marketplace is fiercely competitive. Often that competition may be between agents from the same agency who represent two different performers who are both "right" for the same part. Agents, like all salespeople, have very different sales techniques based on their own personalities and methods of doing business.

The hours are long and the work is very demanding. It is a service business and the agent is expected to be on call virtually at any time to answer the needs, real or imagined, of his client. As with much of the entertainment industry, there is considerable opportunity to prosper financially. Seven-figure compensation packages are not uncommon at the top of the major agencies, and salaries in the middle six figures are frequently found in many of the smaller agencies. Being an agent is not a position for one who covets the contemplative life. Agents receive upwards of 200 telephone calls a day, many of which go unanswered. Meals, weekends, and even vacations are extensions of the workday. The pressure is intense, not unlike the gun-shooter days on Wall Street in the 1980s. It is unquestionably the cutting edge of the business facet of the movie industry. Future film historians will have no knowledge of or interest in how the deals were put together and what powers of persuasion were brought to bear to bring a film into being. Yet for those who like action and pressure, the allure of agency work is irresistible.

To break into agency work, the large agencies all have training programs. Work inevitably begins in the mail room. For a few hundred dollars a week, the trainee is expected to deliver mail, send and receive faxes, and work with senior agents at learning the agency business. That is only during work hours. To escape the mail room, the trainee must work weekends and evenings doing the bidding of some agent whose coattails he hopes to ride. That may entail reading scripts, going to clubs, attending neighborhood plays, whatever the trainee can do to make himself useful. Initiative, stamina, intelligence, persistence, interpersonal skills—all are measured during this apprenticeship. Of the dozen or so trainees, perhaps a quarter will move along, after a year to a year and a half, to being an agent's assistant. This work is principally secretarial—but with a difference. The assistant is supposed to be learning the job. Instruction is given, and day-to-day experience begins to provide insights into the way the business works.

From there, some assistants become administrative aides for an entire department, and then finally get to be agents. The process at a major agency may take four to five years. At that point, there is no limit to the earning ability an agent has. If he signs important talent, that will be reflected in his compensation package. Other perks exist as well, from tickets to films, the theater, concerts, etc., expense accounts, leased cars, and the like. It is a glamorous, fast-paced existence, but not one for the faint of heart.

Life need not be so regimented or highly structured at the smaller agencies. While they often pick up agents after they have been trained at the larger agencies, entry-level positions are certainly not rare among the smaller shops. Since overheads will be smaller, there will probably be a shorter learning period, after which the newcomer will be expected to earn his own way. After a while in the business, the agent will carry his own "book" of clients, not unlike a lawyer or an accountant, which will be likely to move with him should he relocate to another company.

There is another great advantage to learning about the business under the auspices of a talent agency. It can provide the best opportunity to meet the players in the industry—from the buyers to the filmmakers. The agency provides ready access to the highest echelons of the industry. It offers a unique chance to make contacts and establish relationships. For the person starting out, it opens a variety of doors. Many agents are lured to the other side of the desk and move over to buying positions at the studios. In an era where close contacts with stars and directors are deemed an invaluable asset, it is not surprising that agents are considered naturals for studio work. Many agents turn to producing, again building upon their agency relationships. Whether you find ultimate satisfaction working as an agent, or use your experience to move on to other aspects of the picture business, the agency world can be a pivotal step in your career.

In addition to having a talent agent, many performers, and even writers, also retain the services of a personal manager. The manager, also typically receiving a percentage of his client's earnings (from 5 percent to 15 percent, in most cases), ostensibly operates in many of the same areas as the agent. He is not, however, permitted to endeavor to secure employment for his client. By law, that task is solely the province of the agent. So why have a manager at all? Good question. If the world were a more perfect place, probably the personal manager would be superfluous. As it is, the personal manager can be very useful to many performers. In the music business, for example, the manager is often able to be present at concerts and club dates to assure that things are as they should be for the artist, and that the artist gets paid. In the picture business, the manager often rides herd on the agent, ensuring that the agency dedicates all of its energies to furthering the artist's career. Frequently, but not always, the manager enjoys a close personal relationship/friendship with his client and may play a more decisive role in matters of career guidance.

If ego and temperament are removed from the equation, the

manager and the agent function as a well-oiled team in the artist's behalf. They exchange information, consult frequently with one another, broaden the base of contacts, and work to justify the not insignificant percentage of their clients' income that they receive. The manager will probably have fewer clients than most agents and will therefore be able to dedicate more time to his clients. It is rare that the oft-spoken complaint that an artist is unable to get his agent on the telephone is leveled at a personal manager.

In the picture business, some personal managers do what agents are prevented by guild rules from doing—namely, produce their clients' projects. Perhaps they were instrumental in developing the projects for their clients, or perhaps they are simply doing it so as to protect their clients' interests better, but the fact is that it is a frequent occurrence in Hollywood. This possibility offers a unique window of opportunity for the creative, resourceful manager whose clients have the clout to get pictures made. This may be illustrated by the hugely successful personal managers Jack Rollins and Charlie Joffee, who have served as executive producers on all of their longtime-client Woody Allen's films.

Most personal managers received their training in the ranks of the talent agencies. There they learned the business and developed a roster of clients. By personal preference, they gravitated to the management field, which can be very lucrative and, perhaps, less pressured. Occasionally, personal management firms will take on entry-level people and train them to be managers. If the prospect of working in that field holds interest, it is certainly worth the time to try to get into several such companies for an interview.

Another critical member of the supporting players is the attorney. At the early stages of an entertainment career, if one is the client of a talent agency, it is possible to avoid attorney fees by having the counsel for the agency look over one's contracts. Technically, such lawyers are considered business affairs practitioners rather than attorneys for the agency's clients. In practice, however, simple agreements are routinely reviewed by house counsel for the agencies.

Outside the agencies, entertainment business attorneys, especially in Los Angeles, constitute a special breed of lawyers. Businessmen as much as lawyers, they are frequently in the middle of the fast and furious action surrounding the financing of motion pictures, the structuring of the complex deals for the big players, and the constant realignment of the money interests that enter and exit the picture business. It is not uncommon to find the ego of certain entertainment attorneys to be at least the size of that of their clients. This is, in part, attributable to the sizable power they wield in the town. In part, it is a function of the kinds of personalities that are drawn to this kind of legal practice. Not unlike the aggressive prototype of the successful litigator, the successful entertainment attorney wheels and deals on behalf of his client in a major way. He is often teamed with the agent and/or the personal manager to compose a formidable negotiating force on behalf of the client.

It is often difficult to discern clearly the issues that are perceived as the province of the attorney as opposed to that of the agent. When matters have to be renegotiated, for whatever reason, the jurisdictions clearly overlap. Some points, such as the definition of net profits or gross participations, are issues that the attorneys will resolve. Others, such as the making of an overall deal with a single studio, will require input from both the attorney and the agent.

Arguably, for the person considering law school or about to graduate from law school, entertainment practice is a very special branch of the law. It is probably less lawyer-like than most branches of the legal profession. Some understanding of the creative appetites and desires of the clients you represent is important. Similarly, an affinity for the rough-and-tumble business world in which such lawyers function is also useful. Big-time entertainment attorneys are big-time power brokers in the world of Hollywood. They are consulted as frequently as advisers as they are for answers to legal questions. Their contacts span the creative community, the agency and manager worlds, as well as the buyers. Interestingly, in entertainment law, unlike many other professions, the attorneys' contacts among the important buyers, the studios, and the networks go well beyond the business affairs type with whom they negotiate. They are rightfully regarded as stars in this world, and their social and business connections reflect this status.

Many prominent motion picture attorneys have, at some juncture, chosen to abandon their legal practices in favor of joining the management teams of the major studios. Among these are Tom Pollack, formerly a senior partner in one of Los Angeles's most prestigious and powerful entertainment firms, who accepted the appointment as head of the film division of Universal Pictures. Likewise, Frank Wells, now part of the Michael Eisner administration at Disney, traces his roots to a practice of entertainment law. Still others pursue interests in everything from screenwriting to producing when their legal practice no longer brings them enough satisfaction.

For the majority of attorneys, however, the practice of law offers more than enough satisfaction and reward. Most experienced practitioners are flexible as to their method of compensation. That is, they may work for their clients on an hourly fee basis, or, like the rest of the supporting players, shift over to a percentage of revenues earned by their clients. My own experience with the attorney who formerly represented me as a producer is typical. He received 5 percent of my producer-derived earnings from his representation of me. This certainly worked in my favor at the beginnings of deals where my expenses greatly outstripped my revenues. When one picture I produced began to throw off meaningful profits, I went to this attorney asking him to put a cap on his percentage since his firm had more than made up for any billings shortfall. Where an agent would have laughed at me, telling me to read my contract, and that a deal is a deal, the attorney said that he thought that this was very fair and modified our arrangement accordingly.

For the person considering law school and particularly this end of the practice, there are some things to keep in mind. The entertainment community is not the most conservative segment of the business world one could conjure up. You have to have an affinity for the peculiar nature of your clientele and the problems that they will develop. The practice may often resemble personal therapy as much as it does a legal practice. Entertainment practice is singularly pragmatic. Often no one gets paid unless the deal closes, even the attorney if he is on a percentage arrangement. With all of the posturing and temperament surrounding most negotiations, it takes a shrewd and well-balanced approach to steer the right course for your client. Dexterous thinking and an intuitive grasp of the art and science of deal making are often necessary to bring the specific problem to a successful resolution.

Never to be discounted in thinking about a profession such as the practice of entertainment law is the fact that for many it is simply more fun than practicing other kinds of law. It is at once more glamorous and more taken up with interesting people than most professional endeavors. That is a large part of the personal satisfaction that many entertainment attorneys derive from their practices. If that holds little appeal for you, you might cast an eye on some other aspect of the motion picture industry.

Attorneys work, of course, in other than private law firms. There are business affairs and legal departments in agencies, studios, networks, cable companies, and most other good-sized entertainment companies. These positions may not be as freewheeling as their counterparts in private practice, but they offer important experience and contacts. The legal community involved with the motion picture industry is a comparatively small, close-knit one. Any job, especially at an entry level, will expose you to many other people and open up many other doors. Such positions should not be discounted simply because they seem more corporate and less colorful in nature.

When people attain a level of earnings in the picture business that begins to suggest important money, they usually add another member to the cast of supporting players. This individual is known as a business manager. Not to be confused with the personal manager who oversees the client's career, the business manager is concerned only with the tax consequences of earnings and how best to utilize the income and cause it to appreciate. If these job tasks sound like those performed by the standard accountant, of course that is the case. It is, however, the peculiar nature of the picture business, and other high-income show-business pursuits, that has led to the fixture on the Hollywood scene known as the business manager.

Today's business managers are often much more intimately involved in the lives of their clients than simply doing their tax planning. Many clients require nothing less than a strict weekly allowance, with all other money being controlled by the business manager. Major purchases, from houses to automobiles, are discussed with the business manager before the client closes on the deal. This reliance on others to play the role of grown-up to the client's role of child is surprisingly characteristic of many high earners in the picture business.

The successful business managers often control comparatively vast sums of money and are able to put their clients, with their permission, into a wide variety of deals. Like other members of the supporting cast, they too are often compensated by a percentage of the clients' earnings. Given how much the large earners make on an annual basis, this can amount to a considerable sum of money.

While business managers have to reflect some measure of fiscal conservatism and trustworthiness, there is little doubt that they, like other members of the supporting player cast, are drawn to the motion picture world because it peculiarly suits their temperament. They understand the excesses of this narrow segment of the population, and although urging caution, are typically not judgmental. In many cases, they are able to provide services that go far beyond those offered by a traditional accountant. They may be able to effect introductions among their clients, assist in structuring complicated picture deal arrangements, or otherwise work to their clients' benefit.

As a group, they are far too frequently tarred with the stigma of negative publicity when one of their well-known clients sues them charging them with misappropriation of funds. It is suggested that this kind of activity is no more prevalent among business managers for the motion picture community than among those in any other affluent business community. It is only the fishbowl quality of the movie business that makes every alleged wrong leap out at the public from tabloids and other mass media publications.

For the individual whose bent lies in areas financial, and whose passion is motion pictures, the role of business manager might be a worthy goal. The more education you get the better. Certainly being a certified public accountant will help. Having an M.B.A. wouldn't hurt. As has been stressed throughout this chapter, even in the area of business advice this is still a people-oriented industry. Assuming an adequate level of qualifications and expertise, it is the individual who possesses solid interpersonal skills who will succeed in this line of work. Maybe movie people are like any others, but maybe they are not. The high earners are catered to and fawned over in a manner quite unlike almost any other affluent group in the world. Clients get used to not having to do anything for themselves. Their every wish is attended to by someone, and they become dependent on the assistance of others. Certainly, not everyone falls into this category, but enough do that a whole industry of supporting players has come into existence.

Another supporting player commonly found backing up the major performers in the picture business is the publicist or public relations representative. While public relations, as a discipline, is frequently taught at colleges and universities across the country, that highly specialized branch that deals with the representation of talent or the representation of a specific film or theatrical offering is rarely given any mention in academic circles. Notwithstanding this fact, the practitioners in this field are among that industry's highest paid and are staples in the entertainment industry marketplace.

A leading figure in this industry for many years has been Ms. Lois Smith, a senior partner at the New York– and Los Angeles–based firm of P.M.K. With nearly thirty people working on both coasts, P.M.K. is not the biggest publicity firm, but is far from the smallest. Approximately two-thirds of their revenue is generated by the fees paid to them by motion picture and television personalities (or an occasional athlete or celebrity from another field), with the remaining third of their income derived from the representation of a specific film or play. They are charged with developing and supervising all publicity, sometimes worldwide and sometimes only domestically. They are in constant contact with all the media and maintain the steady dialogue necessary to see that the message is disseminated in the manner they wish.

Their approximately 100 individual clients pay around $2,500 a month for their services, with the right to suspend representation for periods when they are not involved in the business. Film projects are sometimes billed to the motion picture studios and sometimes to an individual client who wants them to supplement the work of the distribution company. While such specific film projects have a clearly defined beginning, middle, and end, in many cases, as with Smith's representation of Robert Redford or director Norman Jewison, she has been actively in their corners for many, many years.

P.M.K. is not a union shop, but in places where publicists work full-time for the studios, they tend to be unionized. On the union level, staff is segmented into junior publicists, publicists, and senior publicists. At P.M.K., the division of labor is approximately the same, but the titles are referred to as receptionist, assistant, and publicist. According to Smith, the entry-level salary at a firm like P.M.K. may be slightly lower than at its union counterparts, but progress through the ranks comes faster. Publicists in the Los Angeles area tend to make slightly more money than do those working in New York.

When Lois Smith hires for the New York office of P.M.K., she is not overly concerned with any collegiate training in public relations, which she feels is rarely germane to her field. Since writing skills are important in her work, she has a modest preference for English majors, but does not rule out any other area of academic concentration. She places the greatest importance on interpersonal skills, the ability to get along well with people and to communicate effectively. Since much of her work is spent selling (to media people), she looks for an assertive personality type who is comfortable convincing other people why they should accept the story or message the publicist is paid to spread. As the publicist will ultimately play a role in helping formulate the career goals for his client, Smith also looks to find the kinds of personality that tend to engender trust from other people.

In her field, the best training, she believes, comes from practical, on-the-job experience. By working with experienced publicists and being exposed daily to the deadlines and crises that surround this profession, a reservoir of experience is developed. Add to that some innate sense of good taste and judgment and the result will be an effective and successful publicist. Smith quotes legendary publicist Henry Rogers of Rogers & Cowan in summing up the role of the publicist: "You have to know your client, know your outlet, and have a great sense of timing." Contrary to popular belief, the job is not about spinning a web of lies and foisting them upon the press. Instead, insists Smith, you must convince the press of your judgment and integrity, because you are required to go back to them time and again.

As publicists gain more experience, their value to the firm

and their rate of compensation increases. From an entry-level salary of around $400 a week, someone with initiative can quickly rise to the $50,00-a-year level, and then, in reasonably short order, achieve a salary of $100,000 annually. A firm like P.M.K. also provides commissions for its publicists based on the new business they develop. Overtime compensation, found in union shops, is not a feature of the compensation package at P.M.K.

For Smith, the role of the publicist is very similar to that of the agent, except, of course, that the publicist is not required to find employment for the client. She loves the interaction with fascinating people, the daily exposure to films, plays, books, and media, and the participation in the career planning for clients. She emphasizes that even the assistants are quickly thrown into contact with both clients and the media.

Historically, there has been little if any gender discrimination in the publicity field. Women are paid the same as their male counterparts and have enjoyed comparable success. If anything, opines Smith, women tend to build lasting careers in public relations rather than using the profession as a jumping-off place for other pursuits. Related entertainment areas that have traditionally attracted successful publicists include production, agency, personal management, and studio distribution.

The role of the publicist is an important one in the movie world today. While usually not known to the public except when they are called upon to serve as a spokesperson for their client, publicists are important behind-the-scenes strategizers who position their clients in the most advantageous light with the press, the public, and the industry. They are in the inside circle of the movie business, and their importance as supporting players should not be underestimated.

Beyond the more established supporting players, there are many specialists who provide some kind of support and instruction for the participants and would-be participants in the movie business. On the level of instruction, acting coaches, voice coaches, dialogue coaches, and singing coaches have long been staples in Hollywood. Some are better, even more legitimate, than others. For the individual looking for help in this area, it is always advisable to check out the coaches in as many ways as possible. There are no better recommendations than students, past and present, to determine the bona fides of the coach involved.

For the person seeking to supplement his income by furnishing a service of this kind, Los Angeles may be seen as a very green pasture. There is competition, but if you are good, the word will spread fast enough. Yet it may take a few dollars to advertise and to build a base for yourself. There is no better advertising, after your business is up and running, than word of mouth. Satisfied clients will inevitably lead to more clients. As momentum builds, you will find yourself with all the business you need.

Concerns about fitness have always been a part of the Los Angeles movie world. In recent times, the focus for this activity has shifted from gyms and workout studios to personal trainers. Trainers come to the client rather than vice versa. They design individual programs, encourage their clients to purchase machines for their homes, and have created, in recent years, a highly successful industry. Trainers are not, of course, exclusively the province of the movie industry. No other business will be as responsive to current trends, however. And for the moment, fitness is very much in fashion.

Trainers are one thing. There are also a variety of healing-arts practitioners, masseurs, and others who strive to make minds and bodies healthier, happier places. Sometimes, as when a picture goes on location, what may ordinarily be an individual matter becomes a business matter when someone suggests that the charges be placed against the production budget. This can be a nightmare for the producer and the financier if the demanding party is speaking on behalf of the star of the film. Whatever the expertise of the trainer or coach, the picture business has been particularly receptive to working his skills into its day-to-day routine.

On balance, then, the movie business is more than tolerant of its supporting players. It is encouraging to the point of excess. Certainly a well-structured business arena would find some rationale for eliminating some of these jobs on the simple basis of their being superfluous. That shows no likelihood of happening, and it is safe to assume that the supporting-player cast will remain fixtures in the movie industry landscape. If the job seems potentially exciting and to your liking, pursue it. Do so with the strong conviction that it is most unlikely that any of the supporting-player positions will be phased out in the reasonable future.

THE WORLD OUTSIDE HOLLYWOOD

The movie industry is too frequently thought of exclusively in terms of Hollywood and the feature-length narrative film. There is, however, a vast industry involved with moving images that is quite apart from the films of Hollywood—an industry that encompasses the broadest range of talents, from writers to directors to technicians. These talented individuals are involved in the production of shows destined for other markets. Sometimes, as with network television and cable television, these productions bear distinct similarities to feature films. From budgets to stars to time constraints, they may have different ingredients in their mix. They do offer an expanding market for those seeking employment in production. As such, they offer both a stepping-stone to Hollywood and an opportunity for individuals to fulfill their ambitions, earn sufficient amounts of money, and build meaningful careers.

As we enter an era where films can be known as software, it is very apparent that theatrical releases are far from the only way in which a moving image can be delivered to a viewing audience. The traditional form of movie hybrid known as a Movie of the Week, or simply an MOW, is still alive and well—at least as well as the network television industry from which it sprang. The MOW format is one of television's contributions to the motion picture art form. It is shorter (so as to accommodate the inevitable commercials), made for considerably less money than its theatrical relatives (between $2 million and $3 million instead of $20 million plus), and populated with its own brand of stars who have high television popularity ratings (or TVQs). The subject matter for MOWs varies depending on the current tastes of the viewing audiences. It is not unusual to see cycles such as "The Disease of the Week," or lurid stories given credibility if not respectability by being based on dramas from real life. Social issues, particularly those with highly promotable themes, are also cycled through the MOW time periods in the never-ending quest for high television ratings.

For the creative team mounting these shows, there are some differences from and some similarities to feature films. The writing must follow a prescribed formula so as to leave the television audience panting for more at each commercial break. The lower budgets inevitably mean shorter shooting schedules with less use of expensive special effects. In practical terms, this means that the MOW will shoot roughly twice as many script pages each day as the feature film. Lighting setups have to be simpler and easier to accomplish, directors must "settle" for certain performance levels that they might not otherwise find acceptable, and every technical department from music to makeup must operate under great time constraints. There is even less attention paid to art, under these production circumstances, than there is in feature film production.

But the jobs are there. The shooting schedules will not be as long as with feature films, but the same job opportunities in all facets of creative and technical spheres are present. It is a job market that should never be ignored.

Closely allied with the network television MOW are the cable-company films that also appear first on television world premieres. These films, sometimes made for commercial interruptions and sometimes not, are produced by a number of different cable companies from Home Box Office, to Showtime, to Turner Broadcasting System, to USA, PBS, the Disney Channel, Arts and Entertainment, and the Family Channel. Each concern will have certain fare that it is looking to program for the demographics of its audience. Their needs will change over time, and it is therefore advisable to seek help from the theatrical agent community that covers these companies so as to try to get the right project to the right business entity. The range of subjects that are being sought at any one time is great and some assistance in the selling process is a good idea.

From the standpoint of the technician seeking to break into the production business, it is often easier to get on a cable show or an MOW than it is a feature. Once in the loop, more work will be available to those who distinguish themselves by working hard and seizing initiatives during their first stints. It is certainly less important the title, or even the compensation, one gets when work is made available. The contacts are all-important as they will lead to future employment. There will be time enough to worry about upward mobility once the work becomes steady and your name is in circulation among those who hire technical personnel.

A highly specialized area of film undergoing a major rejuvenation at the present time is the world of animation. Originally in place at all the major studios as a separate production division, animation fell on hard times in the 1970s, with only the occasional Disney film making it to the screen. Television animation was produced in the Far East for cost-saving reasons, and the quality was less than exciting. Today's resurgence finds animation units coming back at the major studios and with important independents such as Steven Spielberg's corporation, Amblin' Entertainment. For the beginner, there are training programs at studios such as Disney as well as educational programs at some of the nation's film schools. From a creative standpoint, there is a virtual explosion of styles from full cel animation to computer animation, clay animation, and other variations. As an art form, animation enjoys a unique place in the motion picture world because of the shelf life of the finished product. Early animation films are not seen solely because of their historical interest, but rather because they tend to be as charming and diverting today as they were when they were first made. With the unparalleled success of

Disney's *Beauty and the Beast* in 1991–1992, as well as the successor offering, *Aladdin*, there is every reason to assume that animation will continue to prosper for the foreseeable future.

Turning farther away from traditional Hollywood fare, there is an enormous industry in this country turning out vast quantities of material broadly lumped under the heading of nontheatrical. Much of this work is done for corporate and industrial clients to serve a variety of business strategies. Most of the work in this field is done in video today, but there are some projects shot on film. Information on this kind of filmmaking can be obtained through the auspices of the International Television Association (ITVA), located at 6311 North O'Connor Road, LB51, Irving, Texas 75039. With more than 9,000 members, ITVA is a useful clearinghouse for information regarding salaries and concentrations of activities in this field throughout the country.

Another resource that provides important information is the International Association of Business Communicators (IABC). This organization serves its 11,000-person membership in a variety of ways including seminars, conventions, and other networking opportunities. Student memberships are available; interested persons should contact IABC at 1 Hallidie Plaza, Suite 600, San Francisco, California 94102.

Most work done in the world of corporate or industrial production occurs on videotape. From the advent of commercial videotape in the early 1960s until today, the growth of this industry and its penetration into the lives of Americans and people outside of America has been remarkable. More than 70 percent of American households owning a television set also have a videocassette recorder. A growing number of those households have more than one VCR. While there are a variety of videocassette formats on which to shoot, the overwhelming majority of recorders utilize the VHS half-inch format. The technology, at this writing, is moving very quickly. High-end and low-end cameras are readily available to the public, whose enthusiastic response has driven prices downward. In the coming years, some pundits have predicted that the next generation of video delivery will utilize HDTV so as to project a full movie screen image with complete clarity of resolution. Such a system might enable a theater to pull an electronic image from a satellite to a dish and then project the image to the screen. This system would do away with the necessity of making prints, maintaining them, and shipping them all over the world. While the HDTV technology is currently in place and has been sampled in Japan, for the moment the costs are prohibitive and it is unlikely to replace traditional exhibition in the immediate future.

For the enterprising individual beginning his career, there are many avenues to explore in videography. The costs are so much lower than film that there are more players in the marketplace. This activity creates more jobs for the newcomer, and the more reasonable production cost will allow the entrepreneurial producer to find some kind of employment almost immediately. The list of different formats that are part of today's video market grows every year as additional uses for this medium are employed. For the person starting out, attention should be paid to opportunities in videos working with public service announcements (PSAs), music, training, corporate image, community relations, annual reports, marketing, fund-raising, point-of-sale display, electronic press kits, sponsored video (or film), or any other special-purpose video for which employment might be available. In the latter category, work can be found doing everything from birthday parties and anniversaries to political bashes. Increasingly, everyone seems to want a video record of important events in his life. The chance to shoot and edit such happenings can often be the sustaining income when the newcomer begins his career.

Many filmmakers shy away from this kind of video activity, preferring instead to make documentaries, experimental films, or other personal film or video statements. This is a world filled with talented filmmakers whose dedication and perseverance often result in truly marvelous films. Theirs is a difficult road, however, primarily because there is so little chance to recoup the investment necessary to make films of this kind. Funded by grants, family money, or interested donors, these films will get occasional showings in film festivals or on cable television. Rarely will they be able to generate enough revenue to return their investment to their backers.

In spite of all the economic difficulties in this area of filmmaking, many of the most talented and most original artists still gravitate to the world of avant-garde filmmaking. The task of writing grant requests is a skill so precise that it is an art form unto itself. When federal and corporate grant money is tight, as it is at the present time, the road to financing these projects can be very arduous. Most practitioners of this kind of filmmaking would certainly wish the money came easier for their projects, but probably would not leave what they are doing for an "easier" kind of filmmaking.

It is possible to get a staff position that is involved in the creation, production, and editing of this kind of nontheatrical material. News programs, national and local, frequently have documentary crews on staff. Other television programming such as "NOVA," "National Geographic," or any number of travel or sports shows work in the documentary format. Occasionally, filmmakers like Frederic Wiseman or titles like *The Civil War* or *The Thin Blue Line* will achieve some considerable recognition from the public. Their filmmakers will then be in the enviable situation of having many choices of projects and films that they are offered the financing to produce. More often, recognition for works in this realm stays within a smaller circle, and the ability to find financing for future projects is as difficult as it is in the world of feature production.

In addition to documentaries, and the previously mentioned video formats, production work is most often found in small production companies whose stock-in-trade is the production of television commercials. Most major metropolitan centers in America have some kind of commercials production capability. Some areas, such as South Florida, owe their status as the preeminent centers of production to the fact that a large number of commercials are shot there annually. These companies tend to use the same people for their shoots, but there is enough turnover that some production work is a very good possibility for the person beginning his career. Such companies also provide ample room for advancement, from both a technical and a creative standpoint. Contacts and experience are the key benefits to be derived from work of this kind. Some individuals find this kind of work so much to their liking that they base their careers in this field. Whether that is your disposition or not, the fact remains that commercials are an excellent place to begin a production career.

One way to explore the world outside Hollywood is to track the careers of several individuals who have begun, or chosen to remain, in this kind of activity. Here are three, chosen from the same geographic area, who represent different ages with different degrees of experience.

Initially, there is Chris Kas, who graduated from the University of Miami's undergraduate film program in May 1991. At this writing, eight months since his graduation, he has begun his professional career in the greater Miami area. While his ambition is to direct feature films, his strategy has been to gain experience and contacts in Florida. He envisions that he will, in time, move to Los Angeles and try to pursue his ultimate goal. In the meantime, he has found work in two nonunion, low-budget features, as a line producer and as a transportation coordinator; in commercials, working as a production assistant and as a driver; and in music video shoots, assisting with the video equipment. He has also promoted his services as a video expert capable of shooting and editing special events. Some work has come to him in this field as well. In this, his first year out of school, he hopes to gross between $25,000 and $30,000.

Kas believes that he is better off beginning his career in Florida than in New York or California. He has determined that while there may be more work in those locations, it would be more competitive, and that he is better served building the credits on his résumé before journeying to another state. In a comparatively short period of time, he will make inroads into the production community and establish enough of a foothold to be able to work with some degree of regularity.

While most of his undergraduate experience was with film, Kas is of the view that both film and tape experience are essential for the technician starting out. He quickly concluded that the video market is far more accessible for the newcomer and that the number of jobs that can be self-promoted is far greater in video than in film. Insofar as the job market is concerned, Kas relies on word of mouth and referrals to keep working. He firmly believes that it is a great mistake to price himself in any way out of the job market. This philosophy has been extended to doing work, on a short-term basis, for nothing so as to get to know a new production company and the people who hire for it. By working hard, he establishes a reputation that, he reports, invariably leads to more work which will be on a paying basis.

Through all of this work experience, albeit at the entry level, Kas has not narrowed his sights to one technical pursuit. He still hopes to direct features. Therefore, all of this job experience is to pile up credits and contacts and, speaking practically, to pay the rent and put bread on the table. This is not always achievable for him in the commercial marketplace. Times may get slow; his contacts may not be working; or he could be defeated by the seasonal nature of production in Florida. To sustain him through the lean periods, Kas aggressively pursues his own video engagements. He also maintains affiliations with a film laboratory where he can do graveyard-shift sound transfers, and with a comedy club where he can do part-time work as a doorman. Such positions may not advance his career, but they will provide much needed financial assistance when things get slow.

Kas has found the life of a free-lance technician to be tough, but not impossible. By dint of hard work and aggressiveness on his part in pursuing leads and networking with production people within the community, he has kept his career moving forward and will generate enough money in this, his first year out of school, to be considered successful. He emphasizes the intangibles in describing his first months in the business world. "You have to want it a lot," he says, "if you expect to get your share of what's out there." He adds that "you also have to be willing to work very hard, without regard to pay, in the early stages of your career." There is a fundamental truth about the picture business, in whatever arena it is played out, in Kas's observation. There are, and probably will always be, more people seeking positions within the picture business than there are positions to fill. That makes it a buyer's market. As a buyer, you can afford to hire the best and the brightest, the hardest working and those willing, at least at the outset, to work for less than important dollars. This is a basic lesson to learn about motion pictures, whether it be in Hollywood or not. Those who don't understand this ground rule about the business, and are not Arnold Schwarzenegger or Tom Cruise, are destined to be disappointed with their progress in this industry.

As for Kas, he assesses the importance of his film education at the University of Miami in relative terms. When he entered the job market, his film degree was viewed with a certain amount of suspicion and distrust based on the number of film graduates who entered the job market believing that they knew everything there was to know and that the world owed them a living. Kas insists that only hard work on his part was able to overcome that particular bias. He does feel, however, that his film education will be invaluable to him when he moves closer to his ultimate goal of directing feature films. He had made student films and worked in all the critical technical areas from camera to sound to editing and believes himself to be well prepared for the challenges he hopes to face in the future. In this regard, his plan is to spend a year or two longer in Florida, continue building his contacts and his experience, and ultimately settle on a film he would like to direct. He hopes, by that time, to have the necessary connections to arrange the financing and be able to direct the project he puts together. If all goes well, he will then make the move to Los Angeles and enter the mainstream of filmmaking, where he hopes finally to make his mark.

Somewhat further advanced in his career, but by no means where he would like to end up, is Tas Salini, who graduated from the master's program in filmmaking from the University of Miami in December 1987. Educated abroad until his postgraduate degree, Salini, like Kas, nurtures the dream of directing features. In the four years since his graduation, Salini has established a niche in the Florida market by producing and directing music videos as well as the occasional music documentary. In this time, he has directed roughly forty music videos and two documentaries. With this amount of work, he has been able to keep his small production company afloat earning approximately $18,000 to $20,000 in his first year and $30,000 to $32,000 in his fourth year. While he observes that the Florida marketplace is very competitive, it is certainly not as competitive as New York or Los Angeles. As with Kas, by dint of hard work and a successful final product, he is able to keep working, establish contacts, and gain invaluable experience.

While Salini didn't necessarily think his life would be built around his entrepreneurial capabilities, the prospect of working for the local television outlets did not appeal to him. He found his niche in music videos and has pursued it as a means to direct feature films one day. At different times, he has imposed deadlines on himself, but has, over the past four years, continued to extend them. He has found that his reputation in Florida has allowed him to continue working and to continue to build his economic base while gaining more and more production experience. All of the work he has done has been commissioned in South Florida. Salini is well aware that there is more work as well as higher budgets available in Los Angeles and New York, but his reputation and contacts are currently located in South Florida. The combination of that plus his low overhead and the essential fact that he enjoys South Florida, have led him to stay in the same area for his first four years in the professional marketplace.

In looking back at his film education and assessing its importance in his earning a living, Salini suggests that his formal training did prepare him for the work he now does. He hastens to add, however, that the rudiments of filmmaking can be taught, just as driving a car can be taught, but expertise comes only after practical experience. With his goal to direct features in mind, Salini now gives himself another two years to work in music videos before he attempts to move on to features. Like Kas, he must always balance the competing goals of earning a living and trying to accomplish his lifelong goal of directing feature films.

In reflecting on the qualities he has found to be critical for success in the job market in which he functions, Salini believes that self-confidence, self-motivation, and discipline have been all-important to whatever success he has enjoyed. He has always believed he had creative talent. Converting that to dollars in a highly competitive market, however, takes a dedication and professional approach that go well beyond talent alone. Without the additional qualities he has developed in himself, he believes that whatever measure of success he has enjoyed could never have been achieved.

Another player, of considerably more experience, in the South Florida nontheatrical marketplace is Raymond McPhee. A summa cum laude graduate of Temple University, McPhee has worked for twenty-seven years in film, videotape, and programs for broadcast and cable television as well as for business, government, science, medicine, and the academic community. He has held executive positions for two major broadcast groups, Triangle Broadcasting Corporation and Wometco Broadcasting. He has also written, produced, and directed more than 200 documentaries and informational programs for all three United States networks and for both international and local television.

In addition to his television activities, McPhee, over the course of his career, has created sales and marketing films, training films, corporate image presentations, and audiovisual presentations for a host of well-known corporate clients as well as government sponsors. His films have won numerous awards for creative excellence both domestically and abroad.

As someone who has dedicated a professional career to the creation and production of nontheatrical film and video fare, McPhee is able to reflect, from a very wide perspective, on the advantages and disadvantages to the filmmaker pursuing this kind of life. Most important to him, his career has afforded him the chance to specialize in what he likes to do, with the freedom to explore those subjects closest to his heart and his intellect. Since he has worked primarily for himself, there have been inevitable slow or down times. McPhee has seized those opportunities to devote his attention to developing the kinds of independent projects and proposals that were of most interest to him. While this entrepreneurial outlook may not fit everyone's agenda, it has been the sustaining force for McPhee over the years.

It is not, he is quick to admit, without its disadvantages. The life of the independent that he has led has an unavoidable sink-or-swim quality to it. As with any independent or small businessman, there is not the same kind of security or benefits that can be found by setting up shop under a large corporate umbrella. He has enjoyed good and bad weeks, months, and even years. When his year meets his expectations, he is able to take approximately $60,000 out of his small production company. He has earned more, and less, per annum over the course of his career. While for him the satisfaction is derived from his involvement with the creative product, he must also wear hats to cover the development and marketing functions for his production company. As he observes, larger production entities will have separate departments that develop and sell projects while the production unit is hard at work on the production and postproduction of previously sold shows. With a one-man shop, all of those roles are essentially performed by him. Add to that the responsibilities of a family and the need for some kind of balanced cash flow to maintain a degree of stability and you have the reality of the life of a small, independent filmmaker.

In assessing his career, in terms of advice to newcomers considering independent filmmaking, McPhee counsels that someone starting out "should be very careful with the selection of his parents." Beyond that, he acknowledges that the entry-level person will find it difficult to make a practical contribution to a production situation. In the face of such harsh reality, McPhee urges that those starting out would be well advised to try to break in with a small production company at whatever job (and whatever salary) they are able to secure. There is a catch-22 quality to breaking into this business, as those doing the hiring are looking for experience in their free-lance personnel, and the only way to get that experience is to go to work. One of the great training grounds for the independent filmmaker used to be local news staffs on small television stations. Today, film is essentially obsolete in television, and much of the feature work has been drastically cut back. The larger the television market, the more positions would be available. (The corollary to that, however, is the more positions, the more intense the competition will be to fill those slots.)

If McPhee were looking for a newcomer to work shoulder to shoulder with him, his emphasis would be on the growth potential of the individual he was hiring. He would be anxious that one day such an employee could blossom into a competent and productive producer, director, or writer. Even with growth potential, the person hired must be able to make some kind of contribution to the production on an immediate basis. There must be an understanding and acceptance that the entry-level jobs will not pay much money, and probably won't produce much in the way of true satisfaction. At that level, work is about doing the bidding of more senior people on the shoot, and doing it willingly and enthusiastically. Since there is always a large pool of people for any available free-lance position, McPhee knows that he can hire those who take initiative in their work and go the extra distance to do more than is expected of them. As McPhee puts it, "I'm looking to hire field hands who have the potential to be Steven Spielbergs."

In terms of what the newcomer should be versed in, there is no doubt in McPhee's mind that knowledge of both film and tape is essential. While most production activity uses tape, the more successful television companies and television commercial companies still shoot on film (although they will probably do their post on video). The more familiarity the person starting out has with both formats, the more valuable he will be in the marketplace. At the early stages of a career, these skills translate directly into how employable he will be.

With his years in the business, McPhee has explored many avenues to try to land production work for himself. At his level, he is not seeking work as crew for other companies, but rather trying to secure a contract for some kind of sponsored project on his own. Initially, to proceed along these lines he must generate a lead. He has, in the past, tried to do this with cold calls to prospective sponsors. Usually, these are based on some concept that he has developed that he thinks will be embraced by a company or an industry. This path to securing work can be long, and often futile, however. Preferable to the cold call is to have enough knowledge about an industry that a network of specific leads is developed. Once some inroads are made into that industry, then it is possible to narrow one's sights to specific referrals. It has been rare for McPhee to find much success in the area of published lists of available contracts (RFPs, or requests for proposals). Too often, in his experience, he finds himself in competition with specialty companies that are already wired into the contracting party. In that situation, all of the time expended in the preparation of a bid is wasted.

When he gets closer to a real prospect, McPhee must usually submit a bid for the job he seeks. Depending on the contract, that may require a budget and frequently also a creative and/or content proposal. Over time, McPhee has evolved software programs that greatly reduce the time necessary to do the budgetary part of the process. The creative component, of course, will take as much time as it takes. McPhee allows that this often puts an unfair burden on the independent, but if he wants to succeed in this line of work, he has no choice but to abide by the ground rules of the system. He figures he will get, on the average, one out of every three bids he submits. He has been at it long enough that he has a good feel for when he is legitimately in the running for such an award. Still, to maintain his position in the South Florida market, he estimates that he submits more than thirty proposals a year. The time factor, from the generation of a lead to the awarding of a contract, will typically run from one to three months.

In looking at his career, McPhee acknowledges that he ended up in Miami, Florida, more by accident than by design. Once located in Miami, he found that he enjoyed the community and wanted to bring up his family in that area. His kind of business could be headquartered in virtually any major city in the country. It is certainly necessary to look at the support apparatus for video and film production before selecting one city over another. Such resources as laboratories, equipment supply houses, postproduction facilities, and a host of other support groups (not the least of which is a pool of competent technicians) are all factors to be considered. Miami, while certainly not the equal of New York or Los Angeles in terms of the critical mass of work done, is still the third largest production center in the country. Such considerations were accorded much weight by McPhee in making the decisions for his career and his life.

There is, then, a large and important industry that utilizes the skills associated with all facets of film and videotape that has nothing to do with Hollywood and the production of feature films or television programs. While this industry, in whichever branch you seek employment, will certainly place great demands on the newcomer, it also offers a good number of jobs, and careers can be established. The experience gained at the beginning of a career can lead in a any number of directions. Almost every career that can be envisioned will have some kind of roller-coaster quality associated with it. There will be good times and bad; times of enormous satisfaction and times of great frustration. For the hardworking and talented person starting out, all of the choices lie in front of you. Nothing is unobtainable, regardless of race or gender. Movement is possible from one area of the business to another, and the opportunity for growth and artistic and commercial success is a constant factor. There is no better way to begin than simply to begin. It is not about shortcuts as much as it is about dedication and hard work. The payoffs are out there; it is only necessary to reach for them.

EXHIBITION

From its earliest days, the movie industry has had three principal components—production, distribution, and exhibition. With the advent of the studio system in the second decade of the industry's history, efforts were made by those with the deepest pockets to control all three aspects of the system. Inevitably, with total vertical integration of the process came the potential for abuse, to the ultimate detriment of independents and the consumer. Hence the Justice Department of the United States government intervened in 1948, entering into a series of consent decrees with most of the major distributors of film. In essence, this had the effect of forcing the film distributors to divest themselves of ownership and control of the movie theaters in this country.

Exhibition then operated at a reasonable arm's length from distribution, and some measure of stability was achieved. By the mid-1970s, however, the Justice Department began to question the necessity of perpetual consent decrees that fell within its jurisdiction. Increasingly they came to believe that any such consent decree should be in effect for only a ten-year period. That attitude, coupled with the pro-business tendencies of the Reagan administration, led the federal government to the view that the consent decrees that operated to prevent joint ownership of distribution and exhibition facilities had outlived their usefulness. This was exactly the kind of encouragement distributors were waiting for. There followed a flurry of buying of exhibitors by the distribution companies. In this seller's market, theater chains were sold for twelve to thirteen times their annual cash flow. Normally, theater chains that changed hands might have carried a price closer to five to eight times annual cash flow. Distribution companies became fearful of losing outlets in major markets and thus not being able to obtain optimum play dates for their pictures. The result was an unparalleled payday for the exhibitors and the beginning of a new era for exhibition.

Many predicted a return to the abuses of the pre–consent decrees period. Others pointed to the fact that the treble damages provisions of the antitrust laws would provide sufficient deterrence to widespread abuses. In actuality, the result of the change in the economic structure of the marketplace has not been as profound as many would have predicted. There are, however, underlying factors that combine to make the exhibition industry something less than a happy place to be at this time.

Until recently, the number of movie screens in this country was increasing annually. Although the total number of screens approximated 25,000, this is somewhat misleading. Many larger theaters have been converted to multiplexes with anywhere from two to twenty screens. The economics of the multiplexes are clear. A common manager, concession stand, projection booth, ticket taker, and so forth can serve multiple screens and therefore multiple audiences. Yet, in recent years, annual attendance figures at the box office have either dropped or stayed flat. Clearly audiences are becoming more selective. They are offered the opportunity to see comparatively recent films on cable, videocassette, and in some markets, on pay television. Curiously, although the price of most other consumer products or services rose inexorably, every nudge upward of the cost of movie admissions was greeted with howls of protest. A ticket price of $25 for a concert or sporting event is taken very much in stride by consumers. But let movie prices move from $6.50 to $7.00 and audiences take to the streets in protest. Undoubtedly the exhibition business should have better handled the public relations aspects of price increases. Competitive amusement prices, increases in the costs of films, and inflation in general would provide more than ample justification for the small increases in theater admissions prices that have been charged. Whatever the reason, the public has rebelled against price increases at the box office, and thus we have the doldrums that currently characterize the exhibition business.

The majority of employees in the exhibition business are the part-time workers with whom customers come into contact at the movie theaters—ticket sellers, concession-stand attendants, ushers, assistant managers, and managers. Behind these field people, there is a chain of command running the operations of a chain of theaters. One of the consequences of the relaxation of the consent decrees has been the consolidation of the business into fewer and fewer hands. Chains became larger and larger as independent theater owners found it harder and harder to keep going. The result has been that there are fewer people employed in the business of exhibition. That fact, coupled with the hard times now facing the exhibition business, means that for the foreseeable future this end of the film industry is not the most promising place for job aspirants to turn.

Above the local theater employees, in the chain of command of an exhibition company, is the home office. Like most corporations, it has a vertical hierarchy. At the top is the CEO, an executive who typically has risen through the ranks to take charge of the company. His tasks are to manage the business, with particular attention to the methods of film presentation at the various theaters composing the chain. Presentation includes everything from a clean theater to comfortable seats to the lamps in the projectors and the sound equipment that each house utilizes. Today's audiences are very sophisticated when it comes to the presentation of a film. Many will seek out houses with Dolby Stereo or THX Sound in order to maximize the moviegoing experience. It is a sad commentary on the state of the exhibition business that many if not most theaters do not keep their technical facilities at a high level. The reason is simple. It costs money to do so, and that money comes solely from the pockets of the exhibitors.

As a producer, I found that any time a film of mine was going to be previewed in some theater with which I was not familiar, I would have to bring in an engineer twenty-four hours before the preview to "tune" the theater. Often the lamp in the projector had outlived its useful life. Or, if the theater had surround speakers, some of them were invariably shorted out. This produced "holes" in the soundtrack or, still worse, static from one or more of the speakers. It was hoped that the acquisition of theaters by the distribution companies would result in better presentation of films. Experience has demonstrated, however, that the desire to keep from spending money takes precedence over catering to the tastes of the more sophisticated members of the movie audience or the filmmakers.

Beneath the director of a theater chain is the film buyer. This individual conducts the ongoing negotiations with the distribution companies for film product. If the pictures he rents do not perform up to expectations, he is charged with effecting settlements to the existing contracts. While some distribution companies today insist that all contracts are firm and require payment according to the terms agreed upon, most allow for settlement discussions to adjust the terms in favor of the exhibitor if the picture didn't perform up to expectations.

Film buyer is an important position in an exhibition company, since it requires the wisdom and experience (and often luck) to predict which pictures will turn out to be hits and which will end up as disappointments. He must pit his judgment and business acumen against the negotiator from the distribution company. From the distributor's standpoint, all films are sure to be box office hits and the exhibitors should therefore pay top dollar to play their pictures. As this will never be the case, it takes a steady and veteran hand to be able to anticipate audience tastes and structure business strategies accordingly. If a theater operates in a free zone, without competition from other exhibitors, the pressure may not be particularly great. For a film buyer working in a competitive zone, however, a wrong move may produce a bonanza for his competition and a monstrous headache for his company.

The exhibitor will also have a film booker, who arranges for the movement of prints among the theaters in the chain and advises the buyer when a film has played itself out and should be pulled. This process is anything but an exact science. If the distributors, or the exhibitors, (or the directors, for that matter) always knew what the public wanted, showing films would be a very easy business. Life isn't that way. There are no surefire formulas or even surefire box office draws. Much of the success an exhibitor enjoys will be based on his ability to predict the big pictures each year, particularly in the peak play times of Christmas and summer.

Other executives who populate the home office of an exhibitor include accountants, a personnel director, and a head of advertising. The advertising executive has the important responsibilities of placing advertising and negotiating cooperative advertising terms with the distribution companies. The exhibitors will concern themselves solely with print advertising, leaving the high costs of television to the distributors. It is interesting to ponder the fact that no page of a newspaper has a greater budget for creative material than does the movie advertising page. Even with this fact, there is general agreement that the layout of the average movie page is a blur of competing graphics and messages that frequently leave the consumer confused and discouraged. Within the business, there is little agreement as to whether the consumer consults the movie page of his newspaper to select a movie or simply to find the time and the theater at which a specific film is playing. Such uncertainty as to the fundamental purpose of movie advertising is one of the more peculiar aspects of the picture business.

The final executive in a theater chain performs a critical role. He heads the major profit center in most theater chains—the concession business. Many, many theaters lose money on their film operations on an annual basis. They stay in business only because of the popcorn, soda, and candy that moviegoers buy. Depending on the location, theaters average \$.85 to \$1.50 per customer at the concession stand. Some go well beyond that. A youth film, for example, can produce much greater concession revenue. What is all-important about concession revenue is that it is not split with the distributor. Unlike the box office gross, which the exhibitor must divide along prenegotiated terms with the distributor, every cent of profit from the concessions is retained by the exhibitor, whose markup on popcorn and soft drinks can run as high as 90 percent. Over the years, the distributors have schemed many different approaches to get a piece of this lucrative end of the business. In the end, it was only by acquiring the entire theater chain that they realized any benefits from the concession business.

Typical of the problems facing theater chains today are those dealt with on a daily basis by the Wometco Theaters of Florida and Puerto Rico. This chain has ninety-six screens in Florida and another twenty-six screens in Puerto Rico. This makes Wometco roughly the twenty-fifth largest theater chain in the country. According to Frank Moreno, president of Theatre Acquisitions Co. (the parent company of Wometco Theaters), both his chain and the bigger chains are not faring well at the present time. Much of the problem he traces to the rates charged by the distribution companies for their product. In a business notorious for its low profit margins, Moreno sees the downward turn in the fortunes of the exhibitors as arising out of the increase in the cost of film to exhibitors. The distribution companies' charges come close to 50 percent of the box office gross. Of course, everything is negotiable. As Wometco controls all the important screens on the island of Puerto Rico, it is in a position to negotiate better terms than it could in a town where there were other screens the distributor could sell to. Significantly, Moreno dates the increases in the cost of films to exhibitors to the time when the distributors began acquiring theaters in the 1980s, after the relaxation of the consent decrees.

For many years the number of screens in this country continued to grow, in part because of the conversion of larger theaters to multiplexes, and in part because of the general health of the industry. After this period of prosperity, the count on screens hovered around the 25,000 level. At this writing, the number of screens is moving in the other direction. Many factors are at work that lead to this tendency. Inevitably, some will point to the quality of films shown. Since the beginnings of the picture business nearly 100 years ago, the periodic downturns the industry suffered were cured by a sudden spate of good pictures. To paraphrase from a recent box office hit, "If you give them good films, they will come." But film quality is only a part of the story. Competition for the consumer dollar remains a constant concern in all areas of the picture business. Sporting events, television, the advent of color television, cable television, and now videocassettes and laser-discs have bred a sense of selectiveness in film-goers not present in the past. The notion of going to "the show" on Saturday night is certainly gone, probably for good. Now, before handing over $12–$14 at the box office (plus money for concessions, parking, baby-sitters), the film-goers feel entitled to know that they are going to get their money's worth. Great sums have to be spent in marketing, especially for the purchase of television time, to make the public aware of the movie product being sold. Then the average moviegoer will want further assurance from some trusted source before he ventures out to the movies. This can come from a critic, or more likely from a friend with whom the moviegoer shares a set of common values—and hence the word-of-mouth phenomenon is absolutely necessary to sustain a picture in the theaters. Certain stars are able to "open" a film. Their presence alone will put patrons in the seats for the first weekend of play time. Thereafter, if the film is to have staying power, or "legs," in the parlance of the industry, it needs a favorable word of mouth. It has been estimated that the word-of-mouth syndrome, at its most effective, will cause half of an audience to recommend that friends see the film they have just seen. Therefore, even successful audience-pleasing films will take some time to establish a solid word-of-mouth campaign.

History has clearly demonstrated that movies are not immune to the economic problems besetting the rest of the country (or the globe). Thus, the recession that has plagued America in the late 1980s and early 1990s has taken its toll on the movie business, and the theaters in particular. With the cost of attending films what it is today, renting a video for several dollars less is a very viable entertainment alternative. Likewise, waiting the approximate six months it takes after theater release for a picture to arrive on cable can offer a most attractive savings to the average family.

In some parts of the country, geography causes specific exhibition problems. The Wometco chain in Florida, for example, has suffered during the first half of 1992 from a lack of rain in the state. If the sun shines, according to Frank Moreno, people in Florida don't go to the movies. When the rain comes, business picks up accordingly.

While Moreno paints a fairly gloomy picture of the state of the exhibition business today, he acknowledges that it is necessary to bring young people into the business. With the Wometco chain, there is a preference to promote from within. That means when openings occur in the home office, Moreno tends to look to those in the field to fill them. Because the starting pay in exhibition is so low, Moreno states that it has proved difficult to get college graduates. An assistant manager at a Wometco theater may make \$250–\$300 per week, plus .05 percent of the concession business. A manager can make \$400–\$500 per week plus 1 percent to 1½ percent of the concession business. Depending on the theater, this share of the concessions can produce a bonus of up to \$12,000 a year.

Executive salaries for a small chain like Wometco are not in keeping with other levels of the film industry. Department heads earn in the area of \$75,000 per year, while film buyers can push that figure up closer to \$200,000.

The business is susceptible to some lateral movement, as good executives in the exhibition business do get noticed and offered better-paying situations with other companies. There is also the possibility, although it doesn't occur often, to move from an exhibitor into the top ranks of a distributor. Warner Bros.' Barry Reardon earned his stripes as the film buyer for one of the country's largest and most successful exhibitor chains, General Cinema Corporation.

For Moreno, the key to advancement within the ranks of Wometco is the kind of resourcefulness that is found in any successful small business. He has favorably responded to recommendations from managers or even assistant managers in his theaters for structural changes in the lobby to permit easier access to the concession stands. He is similarly enthusiastic about managers whose sense of showmanship can bring more patrons into the theaters. In an industry that is not enjoying its finest hour, it is the energetic and resourceful manager who will rise to the top. On the other hand, there are simply not that many openings to be found. As smaller chains were absorbed into larger ones in the 1980s, many executives were permanently displaced. With the exhibition business still undergoing a pronounced downsizing, jobs are not plentiful.

Through all of these changes in theater ownership, the attendance patterns of the American public have remained the same. The average attendance jumps dramatically during the Christmas season and during the summer. In most houses, this increase can be as much as 35 percent to 40 percent of the weekly gross. These are the peak playing seasons, and the marketplace is at its most competitive. More money is spent in advertising and the exhibitors are particularly loath to leave pictures in their theaters that are not doing business. What may be sufficient, on a weekly gross basis, at another time of year will not sustain a film's engagement during Christmas or summer.

The major reason for the escalation in theater grosses during these play times is that schools are not in session. This fact alone transforms a business that does approximately 80 percent of its business on weekends through most of the year, to a business that does closer to 65 percent to 70 percent of its business on weekends and the rest spread out across the rest of the week during Christmas and summer. Typically, summer pictures tend toward the large, star-filled action epics or comedies aimed at the widest possible audience. Every year will produce its share of surprises, however, as "sleeper" films capture the public's imagination. The picture business is filled with unpredictable turns, and this can prove hugely disconcerting to all areas of the industry when picture costs escalate dramatically and box office attendance doesn't keep pace.

The concentration of power in the exhibition business into a few hands has eased problems people have traditionally had collecting from exhibitors. If, by way of example, a small distributor entered into an agreement with a small exhibitor to play his picture in Nebraska, the collection of the money due the distributor could be a significant problem. Usually the exhibitor acknowledged the money was owed, but indicated that life being what it was, it would be a while before it was remitted to the distributor. This put the small distributor, who might not have a succession of other films he could threaten to withhold, in a difficult position. To bring a lawsuit might cost more than the amount owed. And the venue for any court action would be on the home court of the exhibitor. This fact posed additional concerns for the distributor.

With the advent of more and more large theater chains, many of which are publicly traded, the problem of collections is not as severe as it was in former times. This is at least one clear-cut benefit to the process that has been derived from the current trends toward bigness.

If things are not at their most upbeat in the world of exhibition at the present time, what about the future? What can be predicted about the months and years to come in a market segment that has been hit hard by economic times? First it should be noted that with some important exceptions, exhibitors operate their theaters on leases and do not own the land itself. This is significant since it removes one way that the exhibitors could think about cutting back or converting real estate holdings to more liquid assets.

From a standpoint of competition, it is unclear what the future holds in store. Many assumed that theatrical exhibition would not withstand the competition from free television, or later from videocassettes. Yet, the moviegoing experience has survived those entries in the leisure-time-dollar sweepstakes. To a large degree, the most frequent moviegoer became a 15-to-25-year-old. Movies came to be made expressly to serve that audience, even to the extent of pandering to them with the content of some films.

Technology will certainly effect changes in the years to come. Outside theatrical exhibition, the specter of pay-for-view looms large on the horizon. What will American moviegoers do if they can dial or call up a first-run motion picture that is playing day-and-date with the theater in their community? The experiments that have been run to date in isolated communities across the country have not been decisive.

What HDTV, if it is adapted to wide-scale home use, might do to theatrical attendance figures is also an open question. The possibility of seeing a wall-sized image in your own home with theatrical-quality images is a daunting one to today's exhibitors. Those who have predicted the demise of theatrical exhibition in the past have found their "informed" judgments to be grossly inaccurate. Exhibition has always proved sufficiently vital and ingrained in the American experience and has withstood competition from the new technologies.

What of the current methods of presentation? Is there help for an ailing segment of the movie business to be found in this quarter? Perhaps. Film itself may be an outmoded medium from the standpoint of delivering the finished product to the public. Industry observers have speculated for years that the future would be based upon electronic images taken by a down-link in a theater complex from a satellite. Gone would be the expense of striking 35mm (or even 70mm) prints. Gone, too, would be the shipment and handling costs of prints, not to mention the cost of replacement prints. In their place would be the always perfect images captured from the satellite and projected on a high-resolution screen in a modern version of today's theaters.

Whether this is the shape of things to come or not, it does seem clear that improvements in presentations of films are long overdue. The exhibition business has to keep pace with technology, much as it had to do when movies shifted from silents to sound. The public demands cleaner and more comfortable theaters. The growing popularity of such technological improvements in the record industry as compact discs suggests that the public will likewise demand as high a quality of sound from the films they see as they are able to get from the recordings they buy. This puts a demand for capital expenditures on the exhibitors that is unlikely to go away in the future. Those smaller chains that are unable to answer these needs of the public will probably be forced to sell out to larger, better capitalized chains. Maybe then the integration of distribution and exhibition will prove to be a boon and not a menace to the marketplace. Certainly the filmmakers have long clamored for improvements in methods of presentation. They spend long hours building the sound and picture portions of their films. They mix in stereo and employ the finest optical equipment available to bring a technically dazzling product to the consumer. To be defeated at the point of sale by a dim projector bulb or a speaker with a short circuit is just painful.

It is probable that the reporting of the demise of the exhibition business is very premature. There are tangible psychological benefits that are derived from seeing films with other people. Comedies tend to be funnier, thrillers more terrifying, and so on. The means to offer an audience a better movie experience is at hand and is likely to be employed in the near future, if only to try to rescue the exhibition business from its present slump. For the present, most chains are reporting declining annual figures and most chains are for sale. Buyers are hard to come by, however, and the feeding frenzy of several years ago when chains were selling for twelve to thirteen times the annual gross is most assuredly a thing of the past.

For the individual considering a career in motion pictures, it is clear that there are other segments of the industry that are more promising than exhibition is from the standpoint of entry-level jobs and prospects for the future. The next decade will probably see significant change in how motion pictures are presented to audiences. Exhibition will likely shift considerably during that time. If a job seeker has an opportunity to enter the exhibition business at the present time, there could be a unique opportunity to rise through the ranks in a business that is in flux. Change inevitably produces opportunities along with hardships. While it is unclear precisely what shape the exhibition business will take in the years to come, it is a safe bet that some portion of the public will continue to go outside their homes to see movies. That suggests, in turn, that exhibition is here to stay. If nothing else, for the job seeker, it is food for thought.

FILM EDUCATION

We live today in an age of information and education. Success is frequently defined in monetary terms, and education—as in the training of doctors, lawyers, and many businesspeople—is often held out as being a necessary first step to that kind of success. But does the same standard of education apply with equal weight to the motion picture industry? Is some kind of practical training a valid substitute for education? Carried still further, does the ambitious, potentially talented artist "waste time" in formal education when he could be gaining valuable experience working on large films and not learning about them in a classroom or in the production of student films?

These questions represent only the tip of the iceberg. How does one distinguish, when considering film education, for example, between undergraduate and graduate educational programs? Are either necessary, or preferred, and under what circumstances? And, finally, are there different answers depending on what the goals of the individual seeking education and/or experience are? That is, should you develop different answers depending on whether the student wants to concentrate on production or screenwriting?

Surprisingly, there is not a great deal that has been published to assist the individual considering education in motion pictures. If there are no reliable signposts, then answers must arise out of the goals of the individual. To aid in formulating those goals, it may be useful to look at this topic in a general sense before narrowing the discussion to more specific considerations.

Initially, it is a mistake to look at motion pictures as solely the province of Hollywood. The big narrative film that is characteristic of Hollywood's output is only one kind of film activity. Admittedly the most expensive and perhaps the most glamorous, Hollywood product may have only limited appeal to many. Some may favor the more personal films that make up the independent cinema. Others may be drawn to the ever-changing world of documentary filmmaking. Still others, to animation, experimental films, corporate or sponsored films, or music videos, or to any of a number of other forms of expression that use the technology of motion pictures and/or videography. Often the individual's initial choices made in this regard do not become final career choices. Tastes and interests change and grow, and different forms of expression become the new focus of people's energies. The choice of how to get started, then, may not have the cosmic significance that it first appears to have, but it is still a necessary first step. Every journey must start with a single step.

In the early days of the picture business, education was not even a viable alternative. Film was not taught; its skills were just being invented. The founders of the studios and the filmmakers who worked for them were certainly not a traditionally educated group. It has been said of those early pioneers that the reason they were able to judge the pulse of America is that they *were* America. There is much truth in that proposition. From that time to the present, there has been something of a bias against education in Hollywood. Formal education was not a necessity for the pioneers, so why is it needed today? To many, the arrogance of the young filmmaker emerging from film school with a new degree and a still-wet answer print of his student film is reason enough to look askance at all of film education. With the explosion of film education on American campuses in the 1960s, leading up to the present profusion of film classes, both undergraduate and graduate, throughout the country, some of this bias has broken down. In part, this is a result of the many outstanding talents, in all creative and technical categories, who have emerged from the American educational system. In most cases, however, the prospective employer does not attach great significance to a film education and instead cares about his job applicant's ability to get the work done. The lasting benefits of postsecondary education will probably be of little concern to him.

Hopefully, they will be of far greater concern to the recent film graduate. If he has had the benefits of a liberal arts education, with a concentration in film of some kind, it is expected that he will have developed a critical understanding of the world in which he lives that will serve him in good stead for the rest of his life. There is an obvious difference between a technical or vocational school and a liberal arts curriculum with a concentration or major in motion pictures. The student must determine for himself which choice is most appropriate for his needs. Technical training can be viewed almost as an apprenticeship for a designated professional position. The community college or university degree tends to offer a broader education covering more general subject matter. It is not so much a case of one being better than the other as it is a matter of finding the right option for the individual involved.

There are currently more than 650 institutions of higher learning that offer some kind of film instruction. Information about these schools has been compiled by Acropolis Books in its publication *Guide to College Courses in Film and Television.* It is also possible to get comprehensive information from the American Film Institute (AFI) in Los Angeles (2021 N. Western Avenue, Los Angeles, California 90027; [213] 856-7600; fax [213] 962-2119). These film programs range from very large to very small. Some have full production capabilities, while most focus on film studies and perhaps screenwriting. For the student assessing these options, the first task is to decide whether to enter a program that includes production. It is not necessary yet to single out cinematography, editing, or sound as the area of production specialization.

There is also no ranking, at the present time, of the film programs in the country. It is therefore very important for the prospective film student to do some preliminary research into different film programs and preferably visit those schools that might answer his needs. On a national basis, and not considering costs for the moment, it is generally believed that the programs at the University of Southern California (in Los Angeles), at the University of California at Los Angeles (UCLA), and at New York University (NYU) are the most highly regarded film programs. They are the largest programs and have had more prominent graduates than the other schools. Their programs offer all areas of film education, from animation to producing. After these schools, the programs at the University of Miami (Florida), Columbia University (New York City), and the University of Texas (at Austin) are often cited as offering first-rate film educations. This list is certainly not an exhaustive one and may not provide answers to everyone's specific needs (and finances). Indeed, there are always arguments that can be made that smaller programs are preferable to larger ones because there are fewer disappointed students whose films didn't get selected to be produced. Smaller schools may also rightfully pride themselves on having outstanding student-professor ratios, or an extraordinary faculty, or any of a number of important features.

For the student trying to make sense of these competing considerations, it is suggested that he carefully examine the programs at the schools that interest him. He should do this with a particular eye to the focus or concentration of their film program, the equipment they can offer the student during his studies, and the faculty, both full-time and part-time, who will provide the instruction.

Film curricula are typically composed of courses in the history, theory, and analysis of films, courses in production, and courses in a variety of other professional skills—producing, directing, screenwriting, animation. While some programs offer a full selection of courses in all areas, others may specialize in only a few areas.

The equipment that a school has on hand, and whether it is dedicated to both undergraduates and graduates, is also a factor to be weighed. Does the school utilize both film and video? If film is used, will student films be shot in 8mm or 16mm? Are there extra costs, such as film and processing, associated with student film projects, or are all costs borne by the academic institution? What about sound equipment? Or editing machines —are they uprights or flatbeds? What kind of mixing facilities does the school provide? Who owns the copyright on student-produced films? To make your film education a meaningful experience, it is important to nail down the answers to these questions before committing to a school. A firsthand visit including interviews with both faculty and students can often throw considerable light on these areas. Especially important is the chance to speak with students. There is no better source of information about the adequacy of equipment, the effectiveness of program faculty and administration, the frustrations that may be felt in getting films made, and a host of like considerations.

The faculty, too, is extremely important in determining where you wish to attend school. How many individuals make up the faculty? How large are the classes, especially the production classes? What are the backgrounds of the faculty members? Have they come from academia or the professional world, or both? What are their personal areas of specialization? And how many are full-time versus part-time? There is certainly nothing wrong with using part-time professors who are typically professionals taken from local industries. Yet it must be considered that the average part-time professor is probably not going to be on campus and accessible to students as much as the average full-time professor. Again, it is a matter of pairing your desires with the resources of a suitable program. Considerable information is available on educational programs, and it behooves the prospective student to do some serious preparation before trying to make his decision.

Altogether different considerations must be examined if the student is searching out a suitable graduate program. Most graduate programs in motion pictures award either a master of arts (M.A.) degree, or a master of fine arts (M.F.A.) degree. In principle, the difference is that the M.A. is a "scholarly" degree that is an intermediate step prior to obtaining a Ph.D. Thus, the M.A. is usually awarded in the area of film studies. It is awarded after a program of academic classes and the successful completion of a thesis and often a comprehensive examination. The M.F.A., while frequently scholarly in tone, will have a "creative" aspect to it that distinguishes it from the M.A. It is a terminal degree, meaning that it is the highest degree awarded in the creative field. Most film programs offering graduate degrees will award the M.F.A. in production, screenwriting, producing, or a related craft such as directing. The required course work usually culminates in a master's project such as a film or a screenplay.

Why would a student seek a graduate degree in motion pictures? And would it be a help, as in the case of a business degree (M.B.A.) in gaining employment?

Many, if not most, of the students seeking a graduate degree is motion pictures have done their undergraduate work at schools that did not offer film instruction. After getting their bachelor's degree in some other discipline, their choice now is to continue their studies by specializing in film. The same questions can be posed, beginning with the most difficult: is such a student better off going to work and learning on the job, or doing graduate work so as to familiarize himself better with motion pictures and thus make himself that much more desirable to prospective employers? The answer, unfortunately, is again that it all depends.

With no prior film education, and a keen, passionate desire to learn about and make movies, an M.F.A. program may be appropriate. Such a program, usually accomplishable in two to three years, will provide an organized and structured way to assimilate the required information. Of course, the same information can be learned while working in the movie industry, but probably not with the same efficiency or even rigor. To some extent, particularly in areas such as screenwriting, it can even be self-taught. Most students find, however, that some kind of instruction, or, at a minimum, feedback, is a necessary aspect of the learning process. From a production or filmmaking standpoint, a graduate program provides high-level instruction in everything from cinematography to editing to directing. The final-project film will probably aspire to a greater degree of sophistication than most undergraduate films. Thus, the graduate student emerging from a graduate program will have his film under his arm, a considerable background in the study of motion pictures, and a fervent desire to go to work.

It is very unlikely that the student film on which he has spent so many hours (and often dollars) will be able to earn him work. Unless this film wins the Academy Award for short subjects, or is so extraordinary that it instantly attracts money to it, the strongest probability is that it will not prove to be a calling card that guarantees its creator employment. Such graduates must be prepared to begin their careers at entry-level positions working as office help or as production assistants at obscenely low wages and ridiculously long hours. They might be working shoulder to shoulder, at this stage, with high school dropouts who are getting the same pay. The difference, of course, is that the former graduate student is far more upwardly mobile than his high school dropout colleague. He possesses skills and is looking only for the opportunity to demonstrate what he can do. His fellow production assistant will have a much longer road to travel to acquire the knowledge and the skills that the graduate already possesses.

In addition, as the recipient of an M.F.A., a terminal degree, the graduate can, if he wants, elect to teach, either full-time or part-time. For many, this is a good backup option. This is especially true if one's interest has been focused less on Hollywood's narrative films and more on documentaries or other forms of personal film statements. To be able to secure a teaching position in film production may facilitate the making of exactly the kinds of films the graduate wants to make.

Someone with an undergraduate film program in production under his belt, unless he wants the M.F.A. for teaching purposes, should think long and hard before continuing to graduate school. The time and the cost are serious factors to consider. Education is never a "bad" idea to mull over while planning a career. For the aspiring filmmaker, graduate programs offer a continuing opportunity to flex creative muscles and make films. It may be some time before that chance is provided in the real world. Whether graduate school is the right choice is a matter of individual preference.

On the other hand, the situation for the aspiring screenwriter contemplating an M.F.A. may be quite different. Whether he has had some screenwriting in his undergraduate career or not, the chances are he is not yet ready to take his script(s) under his arm and try to earn a living with his screenwriting abilities. It may make great sense for him to work with experienced professors furnishing feedback over the two years that it takes to complete the degree program. Then, with two or three finished scripts, he may be in a better position to get an agent and/or find employment as a writer. As it does for production students, the M.F.A. degree will allow the aspiring screenwriter the option of teaching, which may prove important at some stage of his career.

Some have complained of both undergraduate and graduate film education that you are forced to learn much that is irrelevant to the marketplace and its reality. As a producer and studio executive who came in from the cold to run a film program at a major university, I have some sympathy with this position. You can most assuredly function at the highest levels of the movie industry with, for example, no notion of film theory. Many directors, even at the highest levels, have only a dim awareness of the technical facets of their job as filmmakers. Indeed, directors like Spielberg, Scorsese, Coppola, and Lucas, who are brilliant technicians as well as directors, are something of a rarity. Most directors are nowhere near as skilled with the technology. As far as film theory goes, it is the rare filmmaker today who sees the relevance to his craft of such film theorists as Bazin, Arnheim, Kracauer, or Metz. Why, then, should students be required to explore these theorists and their writings? In part, because it is there. Film theory has certainly made a contribution to the understanding of film as an art form and is, for some, a vital and dynamic part of film studies. Along with the study of film genres, directors, gender, national cinemas, criticism, analysis, and history, film theory does contribute in considerable degree to the student's grasp of the film medium. Comprehensive film programs, both at the undergraduate and graduate levels, will require a liberal sampling of such studies for everyone enrolled—including those in production and writing.

It is not an accident that most of the significant film schools in the country tend to cluster around those geographic areas where the most production occurs. Thus Los Angeles, New York, Miami, and Austin, Texas (a central location in that vast state), all have leading film programs. There is some difference between schools situated on Hollywood's back porch and those in other parts of the country. A larger percentage, but probably not a majority, of those students attending a Los Angeles film program will seek work in the movie business. Much of their educational experience is spent preparing for that eventuality. Perhaps their fellow students at schools more distant from Los Angeles will explore a wider range of options, but perhaps not. Some students have complained about the pressure to "make it" in the industry that creeps into film schools at a time when students might be experimenting with more varied avenues of expression. There is certainly no clear-cut consensus on this point, however.

As far as work in the industry is concerned, what realistic expectations can students hold? Granted that movies are the stuff that dreams are made of, but what of the pressure of putting food on the table? Each year, only a few of the hundreds and probably thousands of screenplays written on the campuses of America are optioned and sold. An even smaller number finally become movies. Yet the skills acquired help the student learn his craft. With continued diligence and talent, many more efforts will be rewarded. The movie industry has always been one in which talent rises to the top. How long that process takes is impossible to predict. There is little doubt that, although some screenwriters can make it after teaching themselves the rudiments of their craft, most benefit very much from a formal program of instruction and feedback—which is the essence of film education. That instruction builds the foundation for the student to go out and further develop and refine his skills.

As for the filmmaker, the director, what are his chances of bursting onto the scene after completing a student film? Statistically, you would have to say not good. In a studio capacity, some years ago, I hired a director named Michael Dinner on the basis of a master's film he had completed for the AFI Conservatory Program. It was a big-budget effort, as student films go, around $40,000. Shot in Los Angeles, it utilized many SAG actors with whom I was familiar. I could, therefore, judge the caliber of their performances, as directed by Dinner, against the standard of previous work that I had seen. The results were impressive, indeed. On the basis of that film, Dinner was hired to direct a film, which came to be called *Heaven Help Us*, for HBO Theatrical Films.

This kind of rapid rise to being an establishment director is exceedingly rare. Each year, by definition, the labor pool of aspiring filmmakers expands faster than the number of films that actually get produced. Recently, the number of films produced annually has been shrinking somewhat, a trend that further complicates the problems for the beginning director. Although the odds may appear prohibitive, it is clear that some will make it. Some will have the talent, and the luck, to get the right chances and to succeed. It is naive to believe this kind of opportunity happens frequently and can be counted on. A realistic set of expectations is preferable. Yet it is important not to become discouraged—not to lose the dream. Equally, you must cling to the passion and persistence that it takes to achieve your goals.

It has often been said that directors have to direct and writers have to write. It is usually far easier for a writer to find the time and the occasion to put words on paper, as compared to the director's being able to run film through a camera. This is still another reason why an undergraduate or graduate film education may serve the needs of an eager collection of people seeking to make a mark in motion pictures. The arts have long been subsidized by patrons who believed in the process and the artists who practiced it. Motion pictures and architecture engender more material costs than any other art forms. Rounding up the necessary funding, even for the least expensive kind of film, can take all of one's energies. Thus it is that film schools can offer a unique training ground for aspiring filmmakers. They can provide the opportunity to flex one's creative muscles and to create films that break new ground, that push on the edge of the envelope. It is an awesome thought, but it is something that is within the grasp of each student who sets out to make a student film.

As for the screenwriting students, those talented, determined writers willing to brave the loneliness of the word processor to create a screenplay, it is also a unique opportunity and challenge. Without the immediate pressure to sell one's work, and without the necessity of satisfying the curious demands of today's marketplace, film schools present the screenwriter with an unprecedented chance to depart from today's formulas and create something new—something that reflects his own viewpoint and his own sensibilities. This is heady stuff, but it is legitimately what film education can be about.

After examining what undergraduate and graduate film education consist of, it still remains difficult to give clear advice to anyone. In the end, much depends on the sensibilities of the individual asking the question. Has he reached a point of diminishing returns with formal education? Then, almost certainly, he is better off heading out into the marketplace and learning about the business firsthand. For others, the benefits of formal education far outweigh any time that may be saved by forgoing an education and seeking to learn on the job. The variables are many, and in the end the choice must be a personal one. Whichever direction one follows, there will be innumerable others who have walked that pathway first. Thus, in the end, it is less which choice you make, and more what talent, energy, and resolve you bring to it.

The analogy of professional sports, and more specifically professional basketball, seems apt. Some few, like Moses Malone, have skipped college altogether and headed straight to illustrious careers in the pros. Most professional basketball players have gone to one school or another and refined their skills so that they could compete against ever more polished performers. Sheer physical talent, at that level, is not enough. Many athletes have the physical skills; in addition, they need the coaching and the discipline to harness those talents; and most of all, they need the individual determination to make it. Without that, they haven't a chance. Any number of first-round draft picks have suffered that fate. Yet for every highly touted first rounder, there is a Scotty Pippen today who comes from an unpublicized and little-known program and simply grows in ability each year until he reaches the pinnacle of accomplishment in the league. In the final analysis, the real indicators for success lie within. Film education may play a useful role in preparing you for a career in motion pictures, but it is not the only way to achieve success. In the end, it is one of several viable choices, any of which may be appropriate for any given individual.

THE FIRST JOB

Anyone who has ever experienced the frustrations of the job market knows that almost any pursuit is preferable to the disappointments and dashed hopes that accompany the search for employment. These problems may be exacerbated in the case of the inexperienced worker seeking to break into an industry. Very little of any relevance to an employer is likely to appear on his résumé. Even with diligent efforts, the job applicant will find many doors slammed in his face. All too often, his earnest entreaties will be met by the suggestion that he needs more experience before he will be deemed acceptable for even an entry-level position. Yet this is catch-22 of the worst nature. How can he work if he needs experience to be hired? How can he gain the experience if he can't obtain a position?

On the face of it, the situation is extreme in the movie industry. There are always many more applicants for positions, at every level, in every area, than there are situations available. In short, the picture business is a classic buyer's market. There is no equivalent to law firms queuing up to hire the graduates of the nation's finest law schools. Likewise, there are no recruiting programs eagerly in search of a current crop of M.B.A.'s hailing from the select business school programs across the country. Instead, at every level, and in every area of specialization, there is an informal hiring policy that somehow arrives at determinations of which people to employ. That this process is at work is reason enough for optimism. Someone will be hired. Someone will break through. The task at hand, then, is to learn how to weigh the odds so as to give yourself the best opportunity to be the one selected.

From a strategic standpoint, the most critical (yet often ignored) thing to do is to see things from the position of the person doing the hiring. What does he require? What is likely to make the best impression on him? It is remarkable how rarely this technique is utilized to obtain a desired job. Not to think the matter through in these terms is analogous to playing out a poker hand as if it were a game of solitaire, or preparing for a sports competition with no attention paid to the other team. What will the prospective employer want to see? What will impress him enough to elicit the job offer?

Before answering that question, it is important to get a handle on the ground rules that underlie entry-level positions in the motion picture industry. First, the work will be incredibly time-consuming; and second, in all probability it will result in disappointingly low salaries. This is a direct result of the fact that it is a buyer's market. If you will not work for the proposed wages, there will be someone in the large line of applicants behind you who will. The employer is certainly aware of this fact. Since it is highly unlikely that you will be indispensable to his operation—at least at the outset—it is a matter of comparative indifference to him whether you take the job or not. All the leverage is on his side of the desk. You will not be in a position to change that. You simply have to ride with the punches and accept the situation for what it is. Remember, if you try to get cute, you are likely to negotiate yourself right out of the job.

When applying for an entry-level position in motion pictures, whether in production, distribution, or exhibition, you will be expected to put your résumé on the table for close scrutiny. Most people breaking into the picture industry come directly from school, or from some other field of employment that proved to be less than satisfying. Chances are that their résumé's will not have major credits that are likely to awe a prospective employer. The well-advised job applicant will not have wasted his college career, however. The closer your work record is to your chosen job pursuit, the better. Internships can be especially valuable both in terms of gaining work experience and in providing an opportunity to secure valuable references. Even if the work is unrelated to the picture business, a record that indicates reliability, industriousness, and professionalism will certainly be appreciated by any prospective employer. This proposition reinforces the idea that the wise student seizes every chance to create a meaningful résumé, even while at school. Honor societies, academic accomplishments, awards obtained, scholarships earned—everything helps to lay the groundwork for a successful résumé. It is worth cultivating relationships with those faculty members whose letters of recommendation may be meaningful down the road. There will still be plenty of time to enjoy the college experience. But especially in difficult economic times, the smart student will take advantage of every chance he has to enhance and enrich his résumé.

It is a given that a submitted résumé must be in a suitable format, without misspellings or grammatical errors. In this era of word processing, there is no excuse for submitting a résumé with even one error. Every city has firms that, for a fee, will design and print your résumé. This approach may result in a graphically interesting document, but it is by no means necessary. Your only concern is to satisfy the employer's sense of professionalism. This can easily be achieved by utilizing your own word processor. There is no advantage to be gained by having a résumé printed professionally, but there is much to be lost if your résumé doesn't comport with professional standards.

Often overlooked in the job-seeking process is the cover letter that accompanies the résumé you send to prospective employers. Again, see the issue from the other person's perspective. All résumés at the entry level have more similarities than differences. Over the years, sitting in studio executive offices, I probably received, on average, five to ten job applications per week. Most were virtually interchangeable. What typically made one applicant stand out from the crowd was his cover letter. This is an underemphasized chance to offer a bit of who you are and, equally important, to demonstrate why the employer should care. Perhaps this is tantamount to taking the first step in convincing the employer what you can do for him—why it is that you are the person for whom he has been searching. Whatever tack you take, you should endeavor to separate yourself from the rest of the applicants, create some sense of your specialness and your potential usefulness to the person to whom you are writing. If your letter is distinctive enough, the employer will make time to see you, whether or not he then has an available position. While you shouldn't venture too far out on a limb, for fear of putting off the reader, you should also keep in mind that this is the movie business and not banking. Showmanship is part of the game. The singular person is far more likely to land a position than is the drone.

Something overlooked all too often by newcomers seeking their first industry position is the fact that the industry is a surprisingly small place. You will invariably meet the same persons over and over again if you end up working in the business for any period of time. For this reason alone, it is good to create a favorable impression with an executive, even if (for whatever reason) you do not obtain an immediate position. Individuals are often hired or get some other tangible benefit as a result of an interview or contact that had occurred previously—sometimes years before. The point is that the networking aspect of job interviews can pay both short-term and long-term dividends. The job applicant is well advised to bear this in mind at all times and not be unduly quick to write off an interview or interviewer simply because it doesn't appear immediately as though a job is in the offing.

The best opportunity to secure a position in the motion picture industry (or, perhaps, any other industry) is through an interview. Meeting face-to-face with the person who will be doing the hiring provides a unique opportunity to show your wares to a prospective employer. There is only so much that can be communicated on paper. Schools, accomplishments, societies to which you belong, and other similar credits may wedge the door open for you, but it is the personal interview that will finally get you the job. Getting a busy executive to see you is never easy. Most executives place interviews with prospective employees, especially those seeking entry-level positions, very low on their list of priorities. Do not be surprised, therefore, if you receive a telephone call, often with very little notice, informing you that your interview has been put off to another time. That should not be taken personally. It is simply the way of the business world. With levelheaded persistence you will eventually be able to see the person you want to see.

Getting appointments of this kind can often be a very difficult assignment. If you have initiated the letter writing process, it is not a good idea to wait for a reply. Again, this should not be taken personally. The task of answering your letter will probably not be a priority item for the person to whom you have written. What you might do is close your cover letter by stating that you will be calling that person's secretary for an appointment after a reasonable time has elapsed—something like two weeks. This gives the executive time to answer, but more importantly, it gives you an opening to pursue if he doesn't. On the other end, at the office of the executive, he may have done nothing with your letter and simply left it on his desk. He might also have given it to his secretary with some kind of notation as to what he would like done. Or, in a worst case scenario, he could have chucked it in the basket. Your calling for an appointment is a reasonable follow-up to any action that has been taken at his end.

One thing the job applicant with little office experience should understand is the role of the secretary. A secretary commonly acts as an expediter or chief of staff for the person for whom he or she works. In this regard, the secretary may serve as a gatekeeper, someone to get past if you are to see the executive behind her. Rarely is it a good idea to try to muscle your way past efficient secretaries. They will have not only more experience than you, but also access to the very person you are trying to see. You are better off using courtesy, charm, and a genuine interest in them as people to accomplish your desired goal. Take the trouble to learn the secretary's name when you call. Don't treat them as functionaries who book appointments for their bosses. Rather, befriend them, make conversation to the extent that time allows, and don't be afraid to provide some token of your gratitude if they are able to do something for you. After all, if you do ultimately get a job with the executive, you'll most likely have considerable contact with his or her secretary.

A secretary who is in your corner can tell you when the best times to telephone will be, can be instrumental in making time for you to see the boss, and can even support your application in ways that you may never be aware of. If someone like that has been helpful to you, a simple gesture like having flowers delivered to the office will win you a supporter and a longtime ally. Turning the coin over, it is equally important to realize that while a secretary may not be able to hire you, he or she may be able to torpedo your application by a well-timed word to the boss. It is foolish to mistreat or be rude to the secretary at the other end of the telephone. The movie business is a small business. You will meet the same people many times over the course of your career. If you build a network of supporters who have nice things to say about you, your career and your life will invariably be richer.

If your letter, résumé, and follow-up telephone call prove successful, you will be given a time for an interview. This meeting is critical, and it should be treated as such by you. First, you have to prepare adequately. On the simplest level, this means learning the precise pronunciation of the name of the person you are scheduled to see. Furthermore, you have to do sufficient research to have a good understanding of the company for which your prospective employer works. If it is public, look at the annual reports for the last couple of years. These are available at libraries and stock brokerages. Whether or not the company is publicly held, you should run through the weekly *Variety* trade paper and familiarize yourself with the company's current business. Since the executive with whom you meet will be preoccupied with current product in release from his company, it pays for you to familiarize yourself with the shape and complexion of the marketplace at that time. Are his company's films doing well? Have there been any box office surprises—good or bad? What has been the critical reception of the recent releases from the company? Is there any current news worthy of discussion? Any big books that have been optioned? Any major stars linked with future projects? Any important directors signed for forthcoming pictures?

This sort of discussion is everyday shoptalk for the person you are going to see. The business often seems to rest on a precarious combination of information and gossip. If you have done your homework and learned the lay of the land, you will be able to put your interviewer at ease and create the impression that you are well versed in the workings of the picture business. Much information can be gleaned by keeping up with Hollywood's trade papers, *Daily Variety* and *The Hollywood Reporter*. They appear five days a week in Los Angeles and are "must" reading for everyone in the business. Typically, the day begins for most executives with a perusal of the trades. Many have the papers delivered to their homes so that they can read them before they even get to the office. Add to those trade papers the weekly edition of *Variety*, published in New York, and you will have a good basis for staying up with the Hollywood scene.

Once you are familiar with the business of the company you're going to see, you can further prepare for the interview by developing questions to ask the interviewer when the moment arises. Most executives respond very well to a bright, inquisitive person who asks thoughtful and provocative questions about the business. You are much more likely to leave a favorable impression by discussing such topics than you are by asking about salary or benefits or hours. You will want to familiarize yourself with your questions so as to avoid the necessity of referring to a card or notepad to read them. You want to present the appearance of someone who is very much on top of things and carries questions of this sort in his head.

Guess what? Your mother was right all along—appearances and neatness do count. Even if the person you are seeing is sporting trendy chic designer jeans and a Polo shirt, you will want to show up nattily attired as if you were working in a grown-up workplace and not in the picture business. Put aside any thoughts that this isn't the real you. If you want the job, you may have to put the "real" you on hold until you have gained a secure foothold in the business. While the person interviewing you may or may not have to check with someone else before finalizing an offer, the fact remains that anyone he hires will be something of a reflection of him, his taste, his managerial abilities, and his interpersonal skills. Give him the opportunity to make what he can view as a safe selection. There is no reason to make him feel as though he is taking a big chance by hiring you. There are always too many applicants available to risk presenting yourself as anything other than the best and the brightest.

How you conduct yourself in the interview may well determine whether or not you land the position you seek. A recent study conducted at Stanford University demonstrated through written exams and subsequent work records that there is an equally good chance of finding workers who will perform well on a job by forming intuitive judgments as there is by trying to select people by more "scientific" means. In interviewing for the movie business, most executives will respond in that gut-level way. They will form impressions based on a number of factors. You can help them make that decision favorable toward you by influencing as many of these variables as possible.

As discussed, it is very important to come across as highly motivated, industrious, and full of initiative. Be careful, however, not to go so far that you appear arrogant. A know-it-all attitude has engendered knee-jerk negative responses from many executives who have encountered this trait in job applicants fresh out of film school. You can be interested, modestly well-informed, and still not come across as an authority on all matters pertaining to the movie business. A thoughtful question that reveals a solid understanding of the fundamentals of the business is often preferable to a speech on how things work, or a discourse on why some film did not work. You have to recognize that the person you are seeing does this for a living and is likely to be far better informed and more knowledgeable than you.

Other aspects of the interview process are not unique to the picture business. It is always a bad idea to appear too needy or to create the impression that you are begging for a job—even if you are really are. Human nature shies away from people in this situation, ironically preferring instead those who seem to be in demand. You will always do better if you can create the impression that you are wanted elsewhere and are trying to determine which situation is the best one for you. While something of a stretch, you may be able to convey the notion that you are "hot," and actually generate some mild pressure for your interviewer to act on your application.

In terms of the conversation in the interview itself, some obvious considerations may be worth mentioning. Put your nervousness to one side and approach the conversation with confidence and a firm belief that they would be lucky to have you working for them. You have done your research and preparation. You are as ready as you were when you studied for an exam in school and knew you were going to get an A. You will want to be careful not to fidget or create other distractions. Maintain eye contact with the person to whom you are talking. This is a sales situation and you are selling yourself. It is an error to be too breezy, and equally wrong to be so serious that you leave the impression that you are not right for the movie business. You will be holding a conversation. That means both parties will be engaged in a give-and-take. Don't be so overbearing that you dominate the conversation. There will be more than enough opportunity for you to make the impression you wish to make.

Remember, you should be discussing matters *with* the other person, not talking *at* him. Mistakes like these may simply arise out of defensiveness, but the disastrous results are the same as if you were always that kind of person.

It is also a mistake, in most situations, to present yourself as being argumentative. Again, there is a fine line to tread. What may be commendable in terms of having a well-defined point of view can be a major flaw if that point of view is seen as overbearing or inflexible. An additional mistake is to overstay your time with the executive you are seeing. His work is on hold while you are in his office. Maybe he has instructed his secretary to hold all his calls, maybe he has chosen to take some or all of them. No matter what, your presence puts even greater pressure on him than he would normally have in his business day. Be conscious of these considerations and balance your need to make the best case you can for yourself against the demands of the clock.

You can do much to influence the dynamics of an interview, but it remains a live performance and many things can occur that you will be unable to anticipate. If you are sufficiently prepared for the interview, you should be able to ride through it, no matter what happens. Pick your spots. Let your agenda of what you want to cover mesh with the agenda of the interviewer so that he always feels he is in control. While it may be small consolation the first couple of times you go through the process, interviewing is a skill and you get better the more times you do it. "Giving good interview" is almost an art form unto itself. A lot is in your head. The job is available; otherwise you wouldn't be there. You have been found to be preliminarily acceptable; otherwise you wouldn't have made it to the interview step. Now you have to psych yourself into believing, truly believing, that you are the best person for the job. In doing so, you'll find that you'll make your own luck.

Many job applicants consider their work over when they emerge from an interview and say good-bye to the secretary. They head out assuming that they have done everything they can do to get the job they are after. This is not the case. Some gesture of appreciation for the executive's having spent time with you is an essential part of the interview process. Usually, this takes the form of a simple note saying "thank you" for taking time to see you. Not only does this demonstrate courtesy and good taste, it also provides another contact with your prospective employer. Hollywood is notorious for being an out-of-sight-out-of-mind town. If the telephone rang as you were leaving the executive's office, his mind was off you and on the pressing problems of the day before you closed the door. A letter from you will serve to keep your name in front of him, where you want it. If some unresolved aspect of your previous conversation can be settled in this letter, so much the better. Even if it is only a traditional thank-you note, a follow-up letter is a very important and meaningful gesture.

As far as additional follow-through is concerned, you will have to be guided by the specifics of the interview itself. If you are told, for example, that no action will be taken for three weeks, it makes very little sense to pester the executive or his secretary before that time has elapsed. On the other hand, staying in contact with the office, under many circumstances, is an ideal way to demonstrate continued interest in the position. Persistence is always a necessary part of the Hollywood success story. Entry-level jobs are no different. Within reason, your persistence will be seen as a good quality to have, but if you go too far, you will become a nuisance whose calls are ducked and whose letters go unanswered. Common sense and a continuing awareness of the sensibilities of the other person are the best guidelines for this situation.

It is impossible to overstate the importance of networking at this stage of the hiring process. Family and friends can often provide the little bit of assistance you need to obtain the position you seek. You may, and probably should, have availed yourself of this network to find out about the existence of the job in the first place. Now that you are in the running for it, don't hesitate to ask for more help. Many people have a natural reluctance to ask family and friends for assistance at times like this. They have an understandable desire to achieve results on their own, as well as a reluctance either to bother somebody else or to become beholden to them. Try to dismiss those thoughts from your head. The movie industry is very much a people business. Part of its being comparatively small and centrally located is the fact that calls on people's behalf are made hundreds of times daily. The network is greatly relied upon in the hiring of executives, actors, directors, and crew members. Because it is a common practice, you should feel it is not an imposition to ask someone to make a call on your behalf. Your résumé will probably include names as references and/or letters testifying to your work habits, skills, and general character. Your prospective employer may wish to contact some of these people directly, but these are not the people who should initiate calls to him. Instead, you would look for people you know who also are friendly, personally or professionally, with your prospective employer. Ask them to call, or write, or both. You should remember that all they can do, at best, is help you get through the door. The rest will be up to you. No one will keep an employee around as a favor to someone else. The supportive words of someone from your network may help in landing a job, but keeping it is solely up to you.

Rarely will the entry-level position turn out to be the dream job you have always hoped to land. Typically, the hours will be long, the salary insulting, and your efforts under-appreciated. It doesn't matter! You will have already accomplished the most important step you will ever take—the first one. The whole world looks different when you are on the inside, rather than on the outside looking in. It can never be emphasized enough that your first job is just that—your first job. It gets you into the loop. It allows you to build your own professional network of people who will be in positions to know what is happening, what is opening up, and where you might look for your next position. To put an obstacle like salary or benefits in the way of obtaining your first position is folly. If you can get the job, take it. If it turns out to be a nightmare, you will move to another position. You will be able to do so from the status of being employed. This makes you more attractive to the next employer you speak to. Not only that, even in the worst of circumstances you are certain to benefit to some degree from whatever job you get in the industry.

The picture business is not a business of twenty-five year stints in the employ of the same company. At every level within the industry, people change jobs frequently. You needn't concern yourself, therefore, with how it will look on your résumé to have held several different positions in your first years in the marketplace. Most people do the same thing. The hard part is to begin the process. From the first job, your upward movement will be determined by a combination of the work you perform and serendipity.

You should always stay open to opportunities that you may never have considered desirable. Lawyers become executives; agents become producers; producers become directors. Movement of a lateral nature takes place all the time. Unless your goal is firmly fixed on a single job, such as becoming a director of feature films, you may well want to remain open to the possibilities of different situations. In any event, you will find it necessary to have a passion for the movie business, if not for some particular job within it. Not everyone who seeks employment in this business will find it. That passion, which may find expression in persistence, is perhaps the best attribute to bring to the task of finding a job. If you have such a passion, success is only a matter of time.

FINANCING

The film project that lacks financing is like the proverbial tree in the forest, falling with no one to see or hear it. It may be the most promising project ever conceived, but without funding, it's just deadwood. This chapter is dedicated to the all-important task of identifying potential sources of funding and getting them to say yes. While the specifics may differ, certain identifiable principles underlie this process and thus have a general application in all situations. As a producer who has successfully raised money from studios, private investors, and businesses not normally involved in the financing of motion pictures, I have seen that there are more similarities than differences overall in the fund-raising process.

As with most forms of investment, motion pictures have to be viewed on a risk-reward basis. In this light, the arguments can be very discouraging. The costs are very large and the possibilities of financial disaster are very great, but there is always the hope of catching lightning in a bottle. The yield from films like *Dirty Dancing* or *sex, lies, and videotape* can be so great that whole generations of investors are inspired to try to emulate their success. There remains, however, the vast cost of motion pictures. The average budget for a studio film is more than $26 million, a sum far beyond the ability of most producers to raise privately. Even the smallest films today cost several hundred thousand dollars, and viewed as investments, these films would have to be seen as highly risky. Looked at as a continuum of risk to the investor, the art forms of motion pictures and architecture are daunting in terms of expense needed to complete the project. Even architecture has a risk factor mitigated by developers and other participants in the construction process. Motion pictures stand alone in terms of the risks presented to the investor.

It is therefore remarkably easy for financing sources to find justifications for turning down film projects. The trick is to lead these sources to positive decisions. The successful path will find the producer (for it is the producer who traditionally performs the fund-raising function) overcoming the many persuasive arguments that can be raised against any film investment and somehow inducing the investor to say yes. In this regard, whether you are dealing with a studio, another form of business, or a private individual, it will finally come down to speaking with human beings across a desk. No matter who finally signs the contract, the dynamics of the meeting between you and a financing source essentially remains a buyer-seller relationship. You are selling and your task is to get the buyer to buy. In the overwhelming majority of cases, the project you have assembled will not sell itself. Packages of breathtaking talent, working at fractions of their usual cost, in an irresistibly commercial screenplay are exceedingly rare. In almost every situation, the risk factors in the deal will be readily apparent to the people on the other side of the desk. Those factors will never disappear. It remains your task to overcome them.

To do so, you will have to earn a high degree of faith and trust. Your credibility, your fervor for the project, and your track record will all be factored into the equation. There are many reasons for "money" to say no, and only a handful of reasons why they would say yes. Certainly they will want to assess the degree of commitment you have for the project at hand. If you are lukewarm about it, don't expect others to jump at the chance to support it financially. It will be your passion that will move them to believe, and to say yes. As hard as that passion may be to define, it is a palpably real phenomenon, and something all investors will recognize.

Along with the passion, the investor will be looking for a healthy blend of business sense and creative enthusiasm. Motion pictures are not widgets. Financial profiles are not drawn by computing the cost of goods sold and laying out a model to ascertain the financial yield. The financial analysis is far more complicated, and the risks far greater. Most investors will therefore need constant assurance that you understand both the creative and the business parameters of the deal under discussion. They will need enough confidence in you to overcome the inherent risks involved in the investment. It should be noted that the difference between seeking money for the development of a project and seeking funding for the production of a film varies only in amount and degree of risk. Both are cut of the same cloth, and both involve the same dynamics between you and the buyer or investor.

The first and most obvious place to turn for motion picture capital is the studios. Their greatest advantage is that they are already set up to develop and finance motion pictures. The importance of this basic fact can not be overstated. Whatever the risks may be, studios are in the business of taking them. As a corollary to this, naturally they will approach the consideration of the project in a professional manner. While there may be many human failings in the course of studio dealings, you are never in the position of having to reinvent the wheel for them; they understand the terrain, the risks and the rewards, and they bring their experience to the decision-making process. In rare circumstance, the studio will become so enamored of the project that it will become the pursuer—and the producer, the pursued. If more than one studio is attracted by the scent of a specific project, the producer will suddenly find the leverage in the deal has shifted to his side. Screenplays like *The Sting* have engendered this kind of heat and subsequently benefitted from a bidding war. The phenomenal prices garnered in the auctions of speculative screenplays during 1989–1990 also represents a variation in the classic buyer-seller structure of the market. For the most part, the producer will seldom, if ever, find himself enjoying that much muscle or bargaining power in negotiations with a studio.

Another advantage to dealing with a studio is that their money, once committed, rarely runs out. There are many problems getting the studio to invest in a picture, but unlike the funds from many private investors, the money will usually remain in place once a commitment is secured. This can be very comforting for the producer.

Many projects are simply inappropriate for studio financing. Films that are too small, aimed at too narrow an audience, or concerned with subjects too controversial or too reminiscent of prior box office failures may not fit the studio mold. Studios are in the home run business. They spend so much money in financing and marketing films that they must look first for those projects that have the potential of becoming high-grossing entries in the global marketplace. The tasteful period piece that may garner favorable reviews but stands to make very little money is of little interest to the studio. Yet funding decisions are made with the understanding that there are exceptions to every rule. *Driving Miss Daisy*, successful play and topflight package notwithstanding, was a difficult film to get financed. The box office results surprised and gratified even its most optimistic supporters. As in any sales situation, it is always preferable to give the buyer what he wants. While the precise bill of particulars is always subject to change, in general it is clear that studios are searching for big pictures that are capable of becoming megahits.

To breach the studio walls, you will probably have secured a meeting with a studio executive for the purpose of making a "pitch." Usually arranged through an agent or an entertainment attorney, a pitch meeting is an opportunity to begin the process of convincing the studio that it should support your project. The more preparations you make for this meeting, the better your chances for success. What kinds of scripts is that studio looking for? Who are the writers, actors, and directors with whom they want to be in business? What are the personal preferences of the person with whom you will be meeting? These questions should not be left unanswered. Your agent, other acquaintances in the business, indeed the whole motion picture infrastructure, should be canvased in preparation for a pitch meeting. Your task is to make it as easy as possible for them to say yes.

Many times the buyer will have qualities that are less than ideal. One present chairman of a motion picture studio is notorious for his short attention span. He can tune out after only a few sentences of a pitch and leave the seller talking to himself. Another recent chief executive was infamous for his inability to read screenplays with any degree of insight or understanding. Though you may wish for other players in the process, this is not always within your control. Likewise, the shape of the overall financial status of that studio, or of the economy in general, will not be in your control. If things are tight at the studio, the decision-making process will tend to be concentrated in one or two individuals. If business is good and profits are high, the ability to say yes, at least for development deals, tends to be distributed more widely throughout the organization. These aspects of the process are not within your control, but there is still a lot you *can* do.

For a pitch meeting, you would be well advised to avoid making these common mistakes:

1. DON'T WASTE THE BUYER'S TIME. Executives at studios work very long hours and still find the day too short to accomplish everything they hope to do. For you to take up more of their time than is absolutely necessary is a big mistake. Make your pitch succinctly and skillfully and leave. If the executive has further questions, he will ask them.

2. DON'T READ YOUR PITCH. You can certainly refer to notes, but there is very little that turns a buyer off faster than listening to someone read a prepared pitch. You've got to familiarize yourself with your material so that you can pitch it successfully. If this takes rehearsing, do so. You are trying to capture your buyer's imagination and interest. Give yourself the best chance you can.

3. DON'T STAGE A DOG-AND-PONY SHOW. Unless you have an animation project or a project that is steeped in special effects, you

make a big error by pitching it like an ad campaign. You are selling a movie. The plot and the characters, together with the creative elements you have or hope to assemble, are what will affect an audience. Those are the elements that should be sold—not displays or other artwork.

4. DON'T SELL YOUR PROJECT BY DISCUSSING ITS MARKETING. Many a pitch has gone up in flames when the seller dragged out marketing materials to convince the studio to finance his film. Studios have their own marketing departments. There will be time enough to interact with them. First, it is necessary to excite the production executives about the creative potential of the film.

5. DON'T BE SO PLIABLE THAT YOU APPEAR WEAK. This caveat is one that takes some degree of experience to grasp fully. The studio executive will want to know that you are flexible enough in your thinking to function well in a collaborative medium. More precisely, will you be easy to get along with in your creative endeavors? If you are too quick to abandon your point of view in the face of every studio suggestion, you will be perceived as being so weak that the studio won't want to do business with you. It is a fine line you are forced to walk. Experience will make it much easier.

6. DON'T WASTE TIME WITH LISTS OF CREATIVE ELEMENTS. The studio has more than enough lists in its possession, covering every conceivable creative category. It is a pointless, time-wasting exercise to review your casting lists and director lists at this stage of the selling process. Of course, if you come to the studio with commitments from creative talent, they should be discussed in detail as they are major inducements to a studio to say yes.

Throughout this process, it is important to keep in mind that the executive you are pitching will probably have to pitch his superior on your idea—and you will not be present for that meeting. You therefore have to organize your pitch so as to provide him with a structured overview, rather than inundating him with details that he will never be able to recall. You do your project justice by summarizing the salient points, both creative and commercial, for the executive. If your project is already in screenplay form, don't take up undue amounts of time describing what the studio will read. Make your time at a pitch meeting count!

Much has been written about the studio business being a matter of who you know. It can certainly be said that relationships are a very crucial aspect of the studio business. Just as in the process of securing a loan, the studio, like the bank, will want to feel comfortable with you and with the deal. Close relationships with the creative executives at a studio can build a comfort level that establishes you as the kind of person with whom they want to do business. Such relationships are forged not only in business, but on tennis courts, golf courses, at parties, and on lunch and dinner dates. For most people, the movie business is a twenty-four-hour-a-day occupation. Nowhere is this more true than among studio personnel. If you take the time to become acquainted with these people socially, then it's likely that the comfort level of your relationships will help overcome the very real risk elements of the project.

If your project in not right for studio financing, it may be better suited to private investors. Most young filmmakers finance their low-budget films by leaning heavily on family and friends. As time goes on, and projects become more expensive, it may be necessary to reach out to others, whether doctors and dentists, clients of broker-dealers, wealthy widows, or some other segment of the investing public. For the filmmaker, private financing provides both headaches and blessings. On the plus side, the filmmaker will enjoy greater creative autonomy than he would with a studio. Private investors usually leave the process of making and marketing the film to the filmmaker. A studio will, of course, take a far more active role. Also, while the risk of getting some kind of distribution for the finished film is much greater, a privately financed film that finds distribution will probably do so on much more favorable terms, thereby allowing for better cash distributions than one would find in the typical studio arrangement.

The opposite side of the private investor coin is the fact that there are few more frustrating avenues of fund-raising known to man. Filmmaking attracts peculiar kinds of investor. Often, it is someone interested in the sizzle or sex appeal of this kind of endeavor. Perhaps he nurtures the desire to see his name in lights, thinks he will meet glamorous members of the opposite (or the same) sex, or simply has money to lose and wants to take a flier. Whatever his motivation, you will have to take the necessary time to find out whether he is for real or simply playing games at your expense. It is often very hard to tell. A few years ago I was raising money privately for a small Western to be shot in New Mexico. I lavished considerable time (and money) on a wealthy rancher who professed to want to invest in motion pictures. I had set up a limited partnership where the shares were priced at $50,000. The rancher had a net worth in excess of $20 million, and my time seemed well spent. At least it did until the rancher finally told me yes, he was coming in . . . for $10,000. While that amount is certainly nothing to sneer at, it doesn't do much for a $1.5 million budget.

This points up the problem with private investing. The amounts of money needed to make a viable commercial film today are so great that it becomes harder and harder to find the money privately. In earlier days when tax incentives existed, the entrepreneurial role was considerably easier. Now, with tax advantages no longer present, it is extremely difficult to arrange private financing on all but the smallest films.

It is a mistake to lump all private investors into the same pile. They may be of very different breeds and require very different handling. A Texan friend has been very successful raising money in Texas and the Southwest. His technique is to arrange a social get-together, serve copious amounts of alcohol, have scantily clad women pour drinks, and show video presentations of films he has done and previews of those he'd like to do.

Experience has shown that his way is highly effective with his potential investors.

Were he meeting with more conservative investment counselors, or attorneys, chances are he'd have to change his modus operandi. You learn very quickly in this game that it is never over until the money is actually in the bank. I sailed into a closing in a lavishly appointed conference room in Century City, California, to sign agreements with a private investor who was the heir to a large hand-cream fortune. Surrounded by his attorneys, accountants, and special motion picture adviser, he actually picked up the pen and lowered it to the agreement in front of him, before developing a case of cold feet and backing out of the deal. Why? To this day, it remains a mystery. The only thing I know for certain is that I was the only person at that closing that wanted this young man to go ahead with the deal. The support team for moneyed people rarely understand the picture business, and even more rarely endorse the investment of significant sums of money in a picture deal.

Another important aspect of moneyed people is that they frequently have moneyed friends. To put it another way, money talks to money. This can be a valuable lesson for the entrepreneur. By attracting the right person(s) to the project, the investor may have the ability and the inclination to attract others from among his friends. Perhaps they have done deals before. Perhaps it is because the investment in film is more fun than most. Whatever the reason, it is a link to additional funds that should be aggressively explored.

For the most part, it will take some initial funding on your part to create the necessary wrapping to make your package acceptable to sophisticated investors. Some lawyers have estimated that it may cost upwards of $75,000 to perfect the rights agreements needed, have the investment papers prepared, assemble a marketing offering, have stationery and business cards printed, and pay for the necessary legal, travel, and business expenses that every venture of this kind entails. This sum can be reduced as circumstances warrant, but there is a minimum amount that must be spent: if you are raising sums in excess of $1 million, it behooves you to do so with an air of professionalism. And that will cost money. You will not have many chances with most qualified investors. For that reason, your package should be prepared and ready for the signatures before any meetings are held. It is a mistake to rush into the marketplace before everything is in place.

It must be noted that the federal government and state governments have laws on the books regulating offerings to the public. Moreover, they have a record of aggressively prosecuting those who violate such statutory provisions. The entrepreneur seeking to raise money from private investors is advised to review his plan with a qualified attorney. There are often ways to accomplish what is sought without the need of expensive and time-consuming registrations. It is always preferable to work this out during the beginning steps of fund-raising and thus avoid serious problems further down the road.

Just as information was a vital ingredient for the preparation of a studio meeting, so too is it necessary to gather information about the motivations of private investors. If the only way to close a deal is to have them built in as executive producer, you will want to give that notion serious consideration. If the investors seem preoccupied with the social aspects of the film business, you may want to check out their credentials before spending much time (or money) on them. Maybe, as with many of the investors in large funds such as Silver Screen Partners, there is a desire to get closer to the action of the entertainment industry, and particularly motion pictures. Maybe spreading a little of the glamour out will go a long way toward making deals a reality.

Whatever the motivations of the private investors may be, the well-prepared producer can ascertain them and try to furnish the desired answers to their questions. Chances are, the investors are betting their money on you and your track record more than on the specific project or the marketplace. The investors must come to believe in you, and you must give them the necessary assurance that you are not a fly-by-night operator. No matter how you describe it, you are still the salesman and they are still the buyers. The more effective your sales tools, the more winning your personality, the more genuine your enthusiasm, the better your product appears to be, the greater the probability that you will close the sale. Discussions are easy to hold. Closing is the art form. Plan your strategy well. Do your homework. Don't stint on the time and effort needed to bring the right package to the table. Then demonstrate conclusively that this project is something in which you hold a passionate belief. With all of this done, closings will follow and you will achieve success in the world of private investors. Rejection and frustration will, unfortunately, be as much a part of your business as any other sales activity. If you have the right disposition, you will overcome these setbacks and eventually get the job done.

There is another place to turn for production funding that has been successfully tapped many times in the past. That is the segment of business and industry that is unrelated or only peripherally related to motion pictures. As might be guessed, this is not an easy source to tap. Especially in difficult economic times, when many industries are downsizing their basic businesses, you had better have a very compelling message if you expect to receive serious consideration from a corporate bigwig. At a minimum, you would be well advised to have some means of gaining entry to the highest levels of the corporation you wish to pitch. The size and the risk inherent in motion picture financing removes it from the province of most middle managers. You will need an introduction to chief executive officers, board chairmen, or influential members of the board of directors if you want any chance for success. If any of these figures express interest, there will be time enough to work with the company's numbers crunchers to see if the deal makes sense for them. Working at the lower echelons first is unlikely to produce any positive results.

Getting positioned with major corporate figures is never

easy. Family introductions are very effective, and personal ties are even better. Mutual friends, lawyers, accountants, and the like are still other avenues to explore. Effecting the introduction doesn't get you your deal. It only affords you a time at bat. The rest is up to you.

With today's economy, it is most unlikely that a corporation large enough to contemplate movie financing is going to move too far away from its basic business. Therefore, to make your case successfully, you will have to show the corporation why your plan fits into its business strategy. Perhaps they manufacture hardware and software in the electronic video games arena. You approach them with a package for a project (and sequels) based upon some kind of hypervideo concept that has great marketing potential in the consumer market. Chances are, you will get their attention when you make your presentation.

In this regard, your concept has to be central to the story and not merely a consumer product to be displayed in the course of the film. In the latter cases, companies can be persuaded to cooperate in the production to the extent of donating products for the production in exchange for credit or some kind of logo placement in the film. This is a long way from putting up funding for the film itself.

If the company is already involved in some aspect of motion pictures—for example, an exhibitor owning a chain of movie theaters—the pitch will probably be a lot more comprehensible. The exhibitor will know the risk and the rewards of production. He can gauge whether there is enough synergy between his business and the production business to warrant his time and money. In the past, such companies as General Cinema Corporation and United Artists Theatres have briefly taken the plunge into production. Their experiments were short-lived, however, and they retreated back to businesses with which they were more familiar.

Other companies as far-ranging as Readers Digest and Bristol-Myers have seen fit to get involved in the world of motion picture financing. Usually they were persuaded by an experienced and charismatic film person that this would be an important profit center for them. What they found out, however, is that the lot of the small film supplier, without a distribution operation, is a difficult one indeed. Furthermore, movies have a way of taking up inordinate amounts of executive time and thereby keeping valuable executives from their more profitable pursuits. This has made it somewhat unlikely that an individual can successfully involve a large company in motion pictures today. What recent years have brought about is a shifting of global resources, with countries like Japan, France, Australia, and Germany putting huge resources into Hollywood motion pictures. Hollywood is one of the great American success stories that, in a global economy, the rest of the world has not been able to emulate. Cars, steel, clothes, electronics—all of these products and many more like them can be styled and manufactured abroad and then sold to a worldwide market. Only American motion pictures have proved to travel well all over the world.

Thus, large and very conservative Japanese electronics concerns have poured billions of dollars into Hollywood in recent times. They hope for a fit with their hardware products and the software generated in Hollywood. Most of all, they hope to amortize their vast investments with profitable pictures and increase in the value of their stock holdings. As of this moment, that hasn't happened. Until it does, you can expect a slowdown in the number of large foreign players entering our marketplace. As concerns the producer or filmmaker starting out, such global moves are probably not in the cards for a while anyway. A major producer and former studio head like Larry Gordon attracted a huge Japanese investment for his company, but his track record and connections within the industry made this possible. Until the economy changes, others will not be as successful.

Hollywood, right or wrong, has survived for many years buying and marketing the stuff that dreams are made of. Little if any formal training was needed for studio jobs, or even producing and directing jobs. It was enough that one had a passion for movies. Today, as other disciplines and other nationalities begin to influence the movie business, it is likely that a different order will be imposed on Hollywood. In part, this will be for the good. Curbing some of the excesses is long overdue. However, if constraints are imposed on the creative process, if film content continues to reach toward formulas and not bursts of creative energy, the very foundations of the movie industry will be shaken, if not toppled.

Wherever possible, it is a good idea to try to keep the financial interests passive. When the limited partnership was the favored funding apparatus, it had at its center the proposition that the general partner would be the filmmaker and would make all creative decisions, while the limiteds would be involved only to the extent of their financial investment. As previously discussed, most studios, most of the time, are not going to give you a blank check and let you spend their money. Yet for the filmmaker who lives within his budgetary parameters, there can be a great deal of autonomy. Different studios and different executives will take varying positions on the amount of involvement they will demand.

Motion pictures are very delicate broths, and too many cooks can easily spoil them. On the one hand, films are by nature collaborative and inevitably represent the creative output of many. Even America's foremost *auteur*, Woody Allen, has said that he will always take a good idea from wherever it comes. But films are usually one person's vision. As with Woody Allen, good ideas are welcome, but finally the vision is his. It is not the studio's, not the actors', it is his. It is too easy for studios to rule by committee, an act that frequently results in the watering down of the filmmaker's vision into something less than it was. This is not a case of "good guys" and "bad guys." Both sides, money and creative, want the same thing—the best possible film at the least possible cost. How that goal is arrived at is a daunting task and lies at the heart of the filmmaking process.

If the road to obtaining motion picture financing seems arduous and full of frustrations, that is a very good assessment. In the early 1980s when videotape burst upon the scene, movies were easier to get financed. The new videotape companies needed product to stay alive and they went out and paid significant sums for it. When the cable companies were not getting product from the major companies, they arranged pre-buy deals with independent producers that allowed many people to finance their movies. These funding mechanisms have essentially disappeared as the market has firmed up. A look at the history of motion pictures and technology suggests that other opportunities for motion picture financing will inevitably arise. The resourceful entrepreneur will seize the moment and turn it to his advantage. It is never the easiest way to go, but for a handful of stalwart souls, it is both satisfying and profitable.

Before leaving the subject of money (which can never really be done in motion pictures), one more technique for financing should be mentioned. For the producer who has developed a viable script, or found an exciting book, it may make sense to team up with an experienced producer and let him run interference for you. Especially if this is a first venture into films, the contacts and track record of an experienced producer may open doors and set in motion a whole new career. If you can bring something to the table such as a book or a script, you have the makings of a partnership. If the picture gets set up, your piece of the pie won't be as big as it would be had the other producer not been present, but at least there will be a pie to divvy up.

This process is often called finding a "*Godfather*," in the vernacular of Hollywood. At times, even the studio will take an inexperienced producer and put him together with a more experienced sort with whom they are already doing business. This can not be viewed as a defeat, but rather as an opportunity to learn. *Rocky* was launched at United Artists in this fashion, and countless other projects have been as well.

While this chapter has focused on money for feature films,

the ambitious filmmaker may experience the need for funding for many other kinds of projects as well. Requests for grants, presentations for corporate films or government films, even commercials, all require the use of someone else's money to come into being. Landing one of these opportunities will always require professionalism and enthusiasm. The professionalism will be reflected in your presentation and package. What may well determine the final outcome is something much more intangible—the passion you have for the project. As someone who has been on the receiving end of thousands of pitches over the years, I have found that if I like the basic project, I will be persuaded to say yes when the passion of the filmmaker grips me. If it doesn't, the filmmaker will be looking for another buyer.

A FINAL WORD

Seen as an art form or as a business, motion pictures, in the broadest sense of the term, offer the newcomer a vast arena in which to explore his creative, technical, or business potential. While it is an industry marked by hard work (and commensurate compensation), most people engaged in it will point out that it is also more fun than anything else they could imagine doing for a living. Many will go so far as to profess amazement that they are actually being paid to do what they love doing.

Underlying the success of nearly everyone in the movie business is something not found in many other industries—a passion for what they do. More than anything else, it is that passion that gives them the will and dedication to keep going when the inevitable bumps occur in their careers.

With passion must come some measure of talent and the persistence needed to allow it to develop. It will take hard work. It will take an understanding of the marketplace. It will also take a continuing outreach to those further advanced in their careers from whom lessons can be learned and help gotten. Motion pictures remain a "people business"; Entry into the industry and advancement through the ranks often depend as much on interpersonal skills as on strictly professional skills.

In this regard, excuses can always be found for the frustrated newcomer who has trouble getting his foot in the door. But the door *can be* opened. In every category, in every area, positions are held by those who began with nothing more than a belief in themselves and a passion for the business they were about to enter. History teaches that it is enough. Prepare yourself for what it is that you want to do, and go for it! Your goals are achievable and the rewards, both professional and personal, will make your journey worthwhile.

NEW YORK CONTACTS

Association of Independent Commercial Producers
11 East 22nd Street
New York, NY 10017 (212) 475-2600
(212) 475-3910 FAX

Association of Independent Video & Filmmakers
304 Hudson Street, 6th Floor
New York, NY 10013 (212) 807-1400
(212) 486-8519 FAX

Black Filmmaker Foundation-East
670 Broadway, Suite 304
New York, NY 10012 (212) 253-1690
(212) 253-1689 FAX

Directors Guild of America
110 West 57th Street
New York, NY 10019 (212) 581-0370
(212) 581-1441 FAX

Independent Feature Project East
104 W. 29th Street, 12th Floor
New York, NY 10001 (212) 465-8200
(212) 465-8525 FAX

International Alliance of Theatrical Stage Employees & Moving Picture Operations
1515 Broadway, Suite 601
New York, NY 10036 (212) 730-1770
(212) 730-7809 FAX

International Photographers Local
Local 644 IATSE
80 Eighth Avenue, 14th Floor
New York, NY 10011 (212) 647-7300
(212) 647-7317 FAX

Make-Up Artists & Hair Stylist
Local 789
152 W. 24th Street
New York, NY 10011 (212) 627-0660
(212) 627-0664 FAX

Motion Picture Film Editors
Local 711, IATSE
353 West 48th Street
New York, NY 10038 (212) 581-0771
(212) 581-0825 FAX

Motion Picture Laboratory Technicians
Local 702, IATSE
165 West 46th Street
New York, NY 10036 (212) 869-5540
(212) 302-1091 FAX

New York Women in Film & Television
6 East 39th Street, 6th Floor
New York, NY 10016 (212) 679-0870
(212) 679-0899 FAX

Screen Actors Guild
1515 Broadway, 44th Floor
New York, NY 10036 (212) 944-1030
(212) 944-6774 FAX

Screen Cartoonists
Local 841
80 Eighth Avenue
New York, NY 10016 (212) 647-7300
(212) 607-7317 FAX

Theatrical Costume Workers Union
Division of Local 22
218 West 40th Street
New York, NY 10018 (212) 730-7500
(212) 768-3887 FAX

Theatrical Wardrobe Union
Local 764, IATSE
151 West 46th Street, 8th Floor
New York, NY 10036 (212) 221-1717
(212) 302-2324 FAX

United Stuntmen's Association
131 West 72nd Street
New York, NY 10023 (212) 799-5433

Women Make Movies
462 Broadway, Room 500
New York, NY 10013 (212) 925-0606
(212) 925-2052 FAX

Writers Guild of America-East
555 West 57th Street, Suite 1230
New York, NY 11019 (212) 767-7800
(212) 582-1109 FAX

LOS ANGELES CONTACTS

Academy of Motion Picture Arts & Sciences
5220 Lankershim Boulevard
North Hollywood, CA 91601 (818) 754-2800
(818) 761-2827 FAX

Alliance of Motion Pictures & Television Producers, Inc.
15505 Ventura Boulevard
Encino, CA 91436 (818) 382-1793

American Cinema Editors, Inc.
1041 N. Formosa
West Hollywood, CA 90046 (213) 850-2900
(213) 850-2922 FAX

American Cinemateque
1717 N. Highland Avenue, Suite 814
Los Angeles, CA 90028 (213) 461-9623

American Film Institute (AFI)
2021 N. Western Avenue
Los Angeles, CA 90027 (213) 856-7600
(213) 467-4578 FAX

American Society of Cinematographers
Box 2230
Hollywood, CA 90078 (213) 876-5080

Black Filmmakers Foundation West
3619 Motor Avenue, Suite 310-314
Los Angeles, CA 90034 (310) 201-9579

Costume Designers Guild
Local 892, IATSE
13949 Ventura Boulevard, Suite 309
Sherman Oaks, CA 91423-3570 (818) 905-1557
(818) 905-1560 FAX

Directors Guild of America
7920 Sunset Boulevard
Los Angeles, CA 90046 (310) 289-2000
(310) 289-2029 FAX

Film/Video Technicians
Local 683, IATSE AFL-CIO
Box 7429
Burbank, CA 91510 (818) 955-9720
(818) 955-5834 FAX

IATSE & MPMO
13949 Ventura Boulevard, Suite 300
Sherman Oaks, CA 91423 (818) 905-8999
(818) 905-6297 FAX

Independent Features Project West
1964 Westwood Boulevard, Suite 205
Los Angeles, CA 90025 (310) 475-4379
(310) 441-5676 FAX

International Alliance of Theatrical Stage Employees
Local 33, IATSE
1720 W. Magnolia Boulevard
Burbank, CA 91506 (818) 841-9233
(818) 567-1138 FAX

International Documentary Association
1551 S. Robertson Boulevard, Suite 201
Los Angeles, CA 90035 (310) 284-8422
(310) 785-9334 FAX

International Photographers
Local 600, IATSE, MPMO
7715 Sunset Boulevard, Suite 300
Los Angeles, CA 90046 (213) 876-0160
(213) 876-6383 FAX

International Sound Technicians
Local 695, IATSE, MPMO
5439 Cahuenga Boulevard
North Hollywood, CA 91601 (818) 760-4681

International Stunt Association
3518 Cahuenga Boulevard West
Hollywood, CA 90068 (213) 874-3174
(213) 874-3159 FAX

Make-Up Artists & Hair Stylists
Local 706, IATSE, MPMO
11519 Chandler Boulevard
North Hollywood, CA 91601 (818) 984-1700
(818) 980-8561 FAX

Motion Picture Editors Guild
7715 Sunset Boulevard, Suite 200
Hollywood, CA 90046 (213) 876-4770
(213) 876-0861 FAX

Motion Picture Association of America, Inc.
15503 Ventura Boulevard
Encino, CA 91436 (818) 995-6600
(818) 382-1799 FAX

Motion Picture Costumers
Local 705, IATSE, MPMO
1427 N. La Brea Avenue
Hollywood, CA 90028 (213) 851-0220
(213) 851-9062 FAX

Motion Picture Illustrators & Matte Artists
Local 790, IATSE
13949 Ventura Boulevard, Suite 301
Sherman Oaks, CA 91423 (818) 784-6555
(818) 784-2004 FAX

Motion Picture Screen Cartoonists & Affiliated Optical Electronic and Graphic Arts
Local 839, IATSE
4729 Lankershim Boulevard
North Hollywood, CA 91602 (818) 766-7151
(818) 506-4805 FAX

Producers Guild of America, Inc.
400 S. Beverly Drive
Beverly Hills, CA 90212 (310) 557-0807

Scenic, Title, & Graphics Artists
Local 816 IATSE
13949 Ventura Boulevard, Suite 308
Sherman Oaks, CA 91423 (818) 906-7822

Screen Actors Guild
5757 Wilshire Boulevard
Hollywood, CA 90038 (213) 954-1600

Script Supervisors
Local 871, IATSE
13111 Ventura Boulevard, Suite 105
Studio City, CA 91604 (818) 995-6195
(818) 995-0894 FAX

Set Designers & Model Makers
Local 847, IATSE
13949 Ventura Boulevard, Suite 301
Sherman Oaks, CA 91423 (818) 784-6555
(818) 784-2004 FAX

Society of Motion Picture & TV Art Directors
11365 Ventura Boulevard, Suite 315
Studio City, CA 91604 (818) 762-9995

Story Analysts Guild
Local 854, IATSE
13949 Ventura Boulevard, Suite 301
Sherman Oaks, CA 91423 (818) 784-6555
(818) 784-2004 FAX

Stuntmen's Association
4810 Whitsett Avenue
North Hollywood, CA 91607 (818) 766-4334
(818) 766-5943 FAX

Stunts Unlimited
3518 Cahuenga Boulevard West, Suite 207
Hollywood, CA 90068 (213) 874-0050

United Stuntwomen's Association
3518 Cahuenga Boulevard West, Suite 206B
Hollywood, CA 90068 (213) 874-3584

Women in Film & Television
6464 Sunset Boulevard, Suite 550
Hollywood, CA 90028 (213) 951-4000
(213) 782-4800 FAX